HOW TO GROW
SQUASHES & PUMPKINS

HOW TO GROW
SQUASHES & PUMPKINS

A PRACTICAL GARDENING GUIDE FOR GREAT RESULTS, WITH STEP-BY-STEP TECHNIQUES AND 160 PHOTOGRAPHS

RICHARD BIRD

southwater

This edition is published by Southwater,
an imprint of Anness Publishing Ltd,
Hermes House, 88–89 Blackfriars Road,
London SE1 8HA;
tel. 020 7401 2077;
fax 020 7633 9499

www.southwaterbooks.com;
www.annesspublishing.com

If you like the images in this book and would
like to investigate using them for publishing,
promotions or advertising, please visit our website
www.practicalpictures.com for more information.

UK agent: The Manning Partnership Ltd;
tel. 01225 478444; fax 01225 478440;
sales@manning-partnership.co.uk
UK distributor: Grantham Book Services Ltd;
tel. 01476 541080; fax 01476 541061;
orders@gbs.tbs-ltd.co.uk
North American agent/distributor: National
Book Network; tel. 301 459 3366;
fax 301 429 5746; www.nbnbooks.com
Australian agent/distributor: Pan Macmillan
Australia; tel. 1300 135 113; fax 1300 135 103;
customer.service@macmillan.com.au
New Zealand agent/distributor: David Bateman Ltd;
tel. (09) 415 7664; fax (09) 415 8892

Publisher: Joanna Lorenz
Managing Editor: Judith Simons
Project Editor: Felicity Forster
Editor: Lydia Darbyshire
Photographers: Jonathan Buckley,
    Amanda Heywood, Patrick McLeavey
    and Debbie Patterson
Illustrator: Liz Pepperell
Designer: Paul Calver
Editorial Reader: Penelope Goodare
Production Controller: Steve Lang

ETHICAL TRADING POLICY

Because of our ongoing ecological investment
programme, you, as our customer, can have the
pleasure and reassurance of knowing that a tree is
being cultivated on your behalf to naturally replace
the materials used to make the book you are
holding. For further information about this scheme,
go to www.annesspublishing.com/trees

A CIP catalogue record for this book is available
from the British Library.

Previously published as *Growing Squashes
and Pumpkins*

Contents

Introduction

Cucumbers, courgettes (zucchini) and marrows, squashes and pumpkins belong to the same family, Cucurbitaceae, which includes many important food plants. Courgettes, marrows, squashes and pumpkins belong to the genus *Cucurbita*, while cucumbers and gherkins are members of the *Cucumis* genus. All these fruiting vegetables are superficially similar, but for convenience they are often divided into summer and winter types. Courgettes, marrows, pattypan squashes and cucumbers fall into the summer category, and pumpkins, butternut squashes and acorn squashes are winter types.

BELOW Cucumbers can be grown either in a greenhouse or outside in the garden.

ABOVE Bright yellow courgettes (zucchini) often have slightly firmer flesh than the more usual green ones.

GROWING YOUR OWN

Picked when they are still young, summer squashes have thin, edible skins and delicate flesh, which cooks quickly. Of this group, courgettes are the most widely grown, and many named varieties are now available in a range of shapes, colours and sizes. Marrows, the grown-up equivalent of courgettes, are easy to grow and a good stand-by in the late-summer kitchen. Pattypan squashes look like miniature yellow, white or green flying saucers. The long, narrow, smooth-skinned varieties of cucumber are the best known, but there are also ridged (outdoor), round and yellow forms.

Winter squashes tend to have tough, inedible skins, dense, fibrous flesh and large seeds. Pumpkins are native to North America, where they are synonymous with Thanksgiving. Small pumpkins have sweeter, less fibrous flesh than the larger ones, which are, perhaps, best kept for making into lanterns. Butternut squashes are large, pear-shaped vegetables with a golden-brown skin and rich orange flesh. Acorn squashes have an attractive, fluted shape and look rather like large acorns – hence the name. The skin colour ranges from golden-yellow to dark green, and the flesh is orange.

Squashes and pumpkins are grown as annuals, and the speed at which they develop is astonishing. From a seed sown in mid-spring under glass, they grow into large

ABOVE Carved pumpkin lanterns are a sure sign that autumn, especially Hallowe'en, has arrived.

bushes or vigorous vines, even in cooler areas. Behind the fertilized female flowers, the bulb of the fruit can be seen swelling, growing larger almost day by day. This rapid growth lends them an exotic quality, which can lead people to fear that they will be difficult to grow. In fact, squashes and pumpkins are not difficult at all, and their wonderful leafy quality and large golden trumpets make them ideal for many situations in the garden, not just the vegetable plot. The trailing forms, for instance, can be grown over pergolas or arbours.

The large forms of marrows, squashes and pumpkins should be raised from the ground as they develop, to protect them from slugs and to stop them from rotting.

HARVESTING

The vegetables are ready for harvesting when they are firm and bright, and feel heavy in the hand. Cut off the vegetables with a sharp knife. Avoid tearing the stem, which might lead to diseases. These plants tend to self-regulate the number of vegetables they will carry, and harvesting them as they ripen will encourage the plant to produce more. If you want a plant to bear fewer, larger vegetables, such as on marrows and pumpkins, remove some of the female flowers so that all the plant's energies are concentrated on the remaining crop.

COOKING

Summer squashes are best eaten when they are young and tender. Courgettes have the most flavour when they are small; the flavour diminishes as they get older and the seeds get tougher. Marrows have a pleasant, mild flavour and are best baked plain or with a stuffing. Pattypan squashes, which taste similar to courgettes and can be steamed, grilled or roasted, will keep for just a few days in the refrigerator. The cool, refreshing flavour of all forms of cucumber makes them ideal for salads or thinly sliced as sandwich fillings.

Most winter squashes can be used in both sweet and savoury dishes. The deep orange flesh of pumpkins can be used in pies, soups, casseroles, soufflés and even ice cream. Avoid boiling pumpkins, as the flesh will become waterlogged, soggy and unpalatable. The skin of butternut squash is inedible and should be removed together with the seeds. The flesh has a rich, sweet, creamy flavour when cooked and makes a good substitute for pumpkins. It can be roasted, baked, mashed or used in soups or casseroles. The orange flesh of acorn squashes has a sweet taste and slightly dry texture. The large seed cavity is perfect for stuffing.

BELOW The seed cavities of squashes can be stuffed with mixed vegetables.

types of
squashes and pumpkins

The colourful skins and intriguing shapes of squashes and pumpkins can lend the garden a slightly surreal atmosphere, but these are useful and versatile vegetables, worth growing for their culinary value. Although they are all members of the same plant family, the vegetables they produce exhibit a wide range of shapes, colours and sizes, and new forms are being continually developed, offering still more interest for the gardener. Despite their sometimes exotic appearance, these plants are not difficult to grow and merit inclusion in the vegetable garden.

Marrows and courgettes
Cucurbita pepo

Although marrows and courgettes (zucchini) are sometimes known as summer squashes, they do not belong to the same species as other squashes. However, they do themselves belong to the same species, and were originally a single plant – courgettes were simply small marrows. Over the years, however, named varieties of both vegetables have been developed, and they are now regarded as different vegetables. This means that, although courgettes, if left on the plant, will continue to grow and can be treated as marrows, the immature fruits of a marrow plant cannot be harvested and treated as courgettes.

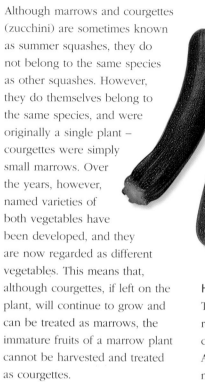

courgettes
(zucchini)

marrows

HISTORY
The history of the marrow is not really known, and although they came to Europe from North America, there are no longer any native species that correspond to the plants we grow today. The marrow reached Europe in the 16th century and has been grown ever since.

The idea of eating immature marrows as courgettes is a relatively recent development.

There are two types of marrows: trailing and bush. The trailing forms throw out long stems that cover a great deal of space, and can be trained over a trellis or archway. The fruits appear at intervals along the stems. Bush varieties are much more compact, and the fruits

RIGHT Pick courgettes when they are small and tender.

grow from the central cluster of stems. They take up less space and are far better plants for small gardens. Courgettes are usually only grown as bushes; marrows are grown as either type.

In recent years courgettes have become much more popular than marrows, partly because cooks have tended to render marrows flavourless by overcooking and partly because, as families have become smaller, a whole marrow is difficult to dispose of in one sitting. However, marrows still have their devotees, and there are some very tasty ways of cooking them.

Courgettes, on the other hand, are not only a more convenient size but, being immature, their firmer texture makes them more suitable for frying, and they are also good for eating raw in salads. Nearly everybody who grows courgettes accidentally leaves at least one on the plant, which develops into a marrow, so there is every opportunity of trying both. The flowers can also be eaten, either raw or cooked.

Marrows were traditionally grown on compost heaps. The heaps or bins were made up during winter and spring, topped with earth and left until the following autumn before being spread. The high concentration of rich, fibrous material meant that moisture and nutrients were in abundant supply, creating the ideal conditions for these plants, and

the heat generated by the rotting compost also speeded up their growth. They can, of course, be grown in ordinary vegetable plots, but using the compost heap does save a lot of space.

VARIETIES

Traditionally, courgettes were dark green, smooth-skinned vegetables, no more than 10–12cm/4–5in long. Now there are many named varieties in a range of sizes, shapes and colours. One of the most widely grown courgettes is 'Defender', a virus-resistant variety which produces early and uniformly coloured dark green fruits. Another early-cropping variety, 'Ambassador', bears long, green fruits, which are easy to harvest over a long period.

'Supremo' also shows resistance to virus. It is an early cropper, continuing to bear succulent, dark green fruits over a long period. The reliable 'All Green Bush' bears dark green courgettes with tender skins; if you cut off the fruits as they develop, new ones will continue to appear. 'Kojac' has a compact, upright but open habit, making it easy to pick the dark green fruits; this spine-free variety is a good choice for a small garden. The fairly new 'Patriot' is a good cropper with well-flavoured fruits; it has some resistance to mosaic virus. 'Sardane' has been developed for its thin-skinned, dark green fruits. It is a reliably heavy-cropping variety, as are 'Bambino' and 'Elite'.

'Tondo di Nizza' bears round, well-flavoured, pale green

courgettes, which are ready for picking as soon as they become golf-ball sized. They are best before they get to 12cm/5in across. 'Greyzini', another quick-growing variety, is a heavy cropper, producing creamy-green courgettes,

BELOW Different shapes and colours of courgettes are available, including long, white Italian courgettes.

which are at their best when 15–20cm/6–8in long but are still sweet and tender when they get longer. The mature fruits can be used as winter squashes. The semi-trailing 'Eight Ball' gives a good crop of dark green fruits. 'Leprechaun', which is strictly a summer squash rather than an immature marrow, should be treated as a courgette. It has bright

green, almost spherical fruits, slightly flattened at the base, with a good flavour and crisp skin.

A variety with plenty of female flowers, the decorative 'Gold Rush' is a quick-growing courgette, bearing a mass of long, slightly curved, golden-yellow fruits. 'Clarion' has unusually coloured, pale green, club-shaped fruits on plants that need plenty of space;

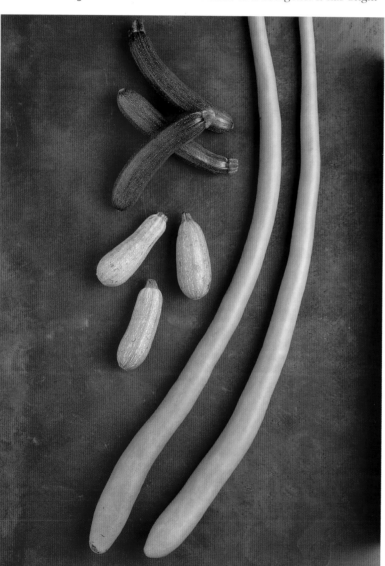

PREPARING AND COOKING

Courgettes need not be perfect – trim the ends and cut as directed.

• To fry courgettes, cook in butter until golden brown, 5–10 minutes.
• Courgettes and marrows can be boiled, steamed or braised in butter with a little stock or water, in a tightly covered pan, until just tender. Courgettes can be sliced or left whole; marrows should be cut into chunks.
• For stuffed marrow, cut a lengthways "lid", remove the seeds, fill with your chosen stuffing and replace the lid. Bake in a dish with a little olive oil, basting often, at 190°C/375°F/Gas 5 for about 1 hour, until tender.

the fruits retain their flavour even if left on the plants. 'Jemmer', which has bright yellow, well-flavoured fruits, is attractive enough for a potager, or even a decorative border.

Among the best marrows are the popular compact form 'Green Bush'. 'Tiger Cross', which is popular with organic growers, is a bush marrow that shows good resistance to cucumber mosaic virus. 'Minipak', also a bush marrow, is a heavy cropper. A good trailing marrow is 'Long Green Trailing', an old-fashioned type of marrow that produces long, green fruits.

NUTRITION

Both marrows and courgettes contain a large proportion of water and hardly any starch, sugar, protein and fat, which means that they are low in calories. They provide some potassium, which makes them beneficial for people with high blood pressure, vitamins A and B and significant quantities of vitamin C. The antioxidants they contain are believed to reduce the risk of some cancers.

BELOW Among the many new forms of courgettes that have been hybridized are some bright yellow ones.

CHILLED STUFFED COURGETTES

Courgettes, like marrows, can be stuffed with vegetables. They are full of flavour but low in calories.

1 Trim 6 courgettes. Bring a pan of salted water to the boil, add the courgettes and simmer until they are lightly cooked. Drain well.

2 Cut the courgettes in half lengthwise. Carefully scoop out the flesh, leaving the courgette shells intact.

3 Dice the courgette flesh and mix with chopped onions, garlic, peppers, tomatoes, capers and herbs. Toss with French dressing and spoon the filling into the courgette shells.

Pumpkins *Cucurbita maxima*

The pumpkin is a curious vegetable. In some arable areas it is treated seriously and grown for the kitchen; in other areas it is planted for fun, to see who can grow the biggest, or it is grown to be carved and hollowed out for a Hallowe'en lantern or mask. Pumpkins are, in fact, often the first vegetable that children grow, because they develop quickly and to such visible effect. Whether they are for decorative or culinary use, pumpkins are definitely worth cultivating if you have the space.

pumpkins, with cross-section showing seeds

HISTORY

Originally from South America, where they have been part of the staple diet for centuries, pumpkins are extremely popular in North America, and it is from there that their recent revival in Britain has come. They are, in fact, winter squashes but are usually treated separately from the other members of the family simply on the grounds of their size and uses. The distinctive name of pumpkin is generally reserved for the large, round winter squashes.

Some people consider pumpkins rather too large for consumption, but not all pumpkins need to be big. The smaller ones, no more than 30cm/12in across, have usually been bred for taste rather than appearance and there is plenty of flesh on them for most purposes. Similarly, not all are the golden colour of the Hallowe'en and show-bench pumpkins.

Since pumpkins grow so quickly, they are good plants with which to encourage young gardeners. The prospect of growing a huge vegetable that will swell visibly day by day, perhaps even becoming too heavy for them to lift, is sure to appeal to children, and having their very own home-grown pumpkins for carving into lanterns at Hallowe'en, as well as making into delicious pies, can only add to the attraction.

pumpkins

VARIETIES

Pumpkins are typically large, bright yellow or orange vegetables, with deep orange flesh. They have a sweet, slightly honeyed flavour and are a great favourite in both North America and Australia. The flavour and texture are not to everyone's taste, however, and some people find them rather cloying, whether used in soups, breads or pies, preferring the vegetables known as English pumpkins. These have softer flesh than varieties from North America. Pumpkin is good in soups, or it can be puréed and combined with potatoes or other root vegetables. Most pumpkins produce large fruits, weighing 8–12kg/18–27lb, but new introductions have tended to concentrate on providing flavour and texture at the expense of size. Generally, new cultivars will produce pumpkins that are flavourful and weigh in at around 2.5–3kg/5–6lb.

'Atlantic Giant' (also sold as 'Dill's Atlantic Giant') is believed to have produced the world's largest

RIGHT The large, bright orange American – or Hallowe'en – pumpkins are familiar to all and readily available during the autumn months. The flesh is ideal for the traditional pumpkin pie.

LEFT The stunningly beautiful 'White Boer' pumpkin has solid flesh that is difficult to hollow out. When carving, use it as a "canvas" for engraving a simple design.

RIGHT The wonderful cushion shape and glorious red glow of the 'Rouge Vif d'Etampes' pumpkin, combined with its easy-to-carve flesh and skin, makes it a perfect candidate for decoration.

PREPARING AND COOKING

Cut the pumpkin in half using a large sharp knife and scoop out the seeds and fibrous parts with a spoon.

Cut the pumpkin into large chunks, then carefully remove the skin using a sharp knife (unless baking).

• To steam, cook cubes in a steamer over boiling water until tender.
• To bake, cut in serving pieces, leaving on the rind, and score the flesh. Arrange cut side up in a greased baking dish and bake at 190°C/375°F/Gas 5 until tender, about 45 minutes.
• To boil, drop pieces in boiling salted water, then simmer until tender, 4–5 minutes.
• To braise, cook cubes with 25g/1oz/2 tbsp butter and a little stock or water, tightly covered, until tender, 4–5 minutes.

pumpkin, one specimen growing to a weight of more than 480kg/ 1,060lb. This is the variety to choose if you are interested in exhibiting garden produce, and the yellowish-orange flesh of modest-sized specimens is excellent in pumpkin pie. Smaller pumpkins tend to have more palatable flesh, and 'Baby Bear' and 'Becky' both produce well-flavoured fruits that grow to 10–15cm/4–6in across. 'Triple Treat' is similar to 'Baby Bear' but slightly larger. 'Jack Be Little' has small, sweet fruits, about 10cm/4in in diameter. 'Hallowe'en' (also known as 'Sunny') bears medium-sized fruits and is an ideal choice for carving into lanterns.

BELOW Although large pumpkins are eye-catching, smaller ones usually have a better flavour and texture.

'Crown Prince' has bluish-grey skin and grows to about 30cm/12in across. The dense, well-textured flesh, which is a deep golden-orange, tastes delicious when cooked, and the picked pumpkins will store better than some of the larger varieties.

'Rouge Vif d'Etampes' ('Cinderella') is a traditional French pumpkin with well-flavoured flesh. The rich orange-red skin is deeply ribbed, and each plant will bear up to four large pumpkins weighing about 4kg/10lb each – especially well-fed plants might even bear pumpkins weighing up to 20kg/45lb each. They will keep for several months after picking.

NUTRITION

Pumpkins are a good source of vitamins A, C and E, and they also contain beta carotene and potassium. Beta carotene and vitamin E are antioxidants and are believed to help reduce the incidence of some kinds of cancer. They contain a moderate amount of starch but very little fat, and they also have a diuretic and a laxative effect.

Pumpkin seeds contain about 45 per cent unsaturated fat, 25 per cent protein, significant amounts of minerals, including zinc and iron, and the vitamin B complex. They make a nutritious snack eaten raw, or they can be toasted or fried. When they are tossed in a little sesame seed oil or soy sauce, they can be stirred into a mixed leaf or rice salad. Pumpkin seeds are widely used in South American cooking, when they are often roasted and ground to make into sauces, or simply sprinkled over salads or other dishes.

PUMPKIN PIE

1 To make the pastry, rub together 175g/6oz/1½ cups sifted plain (all-purpose) flour and 115g/4oz/½ cup butter with a pinch of salt. Add 10ml/2 tsp caster (superfine) sugar and 1 egg, lightly beaten. Mix to a dough and wrap in clear film (plastic wrap). Chill for 30 minutes.

2 Halve a pumpkin, peel and scoop out the seeds. Dice the flesh, put in a pan with enough boiling water to cover, and simmer, covered, for 15 minutes. Remove the lid, add a 2.5cm/1in piece of fresh root ginger, peeled and grated, and cook for a further 5 minutes until all the liquid has evaporated and the pumpkin is tender. Cool slightly, then purée in a food processor until smooth.

3 Roll out the pastry and use to line a 23cm/9in flan tin (pie pan). Gather up the trimmings, re-roll them firmly, then cut them into maple leaf shapes. Brush the edges of the pastry case with a little lightly beaten egg and attach the maple leaf shapes at regular intervals to make a decorative rim. Cover with clear film and chill in the refrigerator for 30 minutes.

4 Put a heavy baking sheet in the oven and preheat to 200°C/400°F/Gas 6. Prick the pastry base with a fork, line with foil or baking parchment and fill with baking beans. When the oven is hot, place on the hot baking sheet and bake blind for 12 minutes.

5 Remove the foil and beans and bake for a further 5 minutes. Brush the base of the pastry case with beaten egg and return to the oven for about 3 minutes. Reset the oven to 180°C/350°F/Gas 4.

6 Mix 200g/7oz/scant 1 cup of the pumpkin purée with 120ml/4fl oz/½ cup double (heavy) cream, 90ml/6 tbsp maple syrup, 45ml/3 tbsp light muscovado (molasses) sugar, 3 lightly beaten eggs, 30ml/2 tbsp brandy and 1.5ml/¼ tsp grated nutmeg. (Any remaining purée can be frozen and used in soup.) Bake for about 30 minutes, or until the filling is lightly set. Cool slightly, then serve with cream.

Squashes *Cucurbita maxima*

The word squash can be applied to a large group of vegetables, some grown as summer crops, others for winter. The word actually also includes the closely related marrows and courgettes (zucchini), which are sometimes known as summer squashes, and pumpkins, which are the same species as squashes but generally thought of as winter squashes. In addition, there are numerous other types of squashes, both summer and winter varieties, so when you are buying seeds or plantlets from a garden centre, make sure you know what you are getting.

The main difference between summer squashes and winter squashes is that winter squashes will store for long periods in winter, whereas summer squashes are for more immediate use, although they will keep for a few weeks. In some catalogues, pumpkins and squashes tend to merge together, and it is sometimes difficult to know if a specific variety is one or the other. In reality, it does not matter: the growing and the eating are the same.

VARIETIES	
Summer	**Winter**
'Custard White'	'Black Forest'
'Dawn'	'Blue Ballet'
'Delicata'	'Blue Hubbard'
'Dixie'	'Buttercup'
'Fancycrook'	'Butternut'
'Little Gem'	'Cobnut'
'Orangetti'	'Cream of the Crop'
'Peter Pan'	'Early Acorn'
'Pink Banana'	'Gold Nugget'
'Scallopini'	'Golden Hubbard'
'Sunburst'	'Green Hubbard'
'Sundance'	'Red Kuri'
'Table Ace'	'Sprinter'
'Table Gold'	'Stripetti'
'Tivoli'	'Sweet Dumpling'
'Vegetable Spaghetti'	'Sweet Mama'
'White Ruffles'	'Turk's Turban'

Squashes are a diverse group of plants, and many of them exhibit weird shapes. Some have crooked necks or look like a Turkish turban or even a flying saucer, while others have ribbed or warty surfaces. The flesh ranges in colour from almost white to deep orange. The taste also varies, but, like vegetable marrows, the flavour is not particularly intense. Although they have some culinary value, they are often grown for their appearance, the wide range of shapes and colours making them both attractive and intriguing.

HISTORY

Originally from South America, squashes were introduced to Europe by returning conquistadors and explorers in the 16th century.

butternut, acorn and pattypan squashes

The majority of the vast range of varieties have been developed in South and North America, and it is only recently that they have regained popularity in Britain.

VARIETIES

Acorn squashes are small and heart-shaped, usually with a deep green or orange skin. They can be cooked in the same ways as pumpkins or baked whole, split in half and served with butter. Varieties include 'Table Ace', which produces dark green fruits on short vines, and 'Table Gold', a semi-bush variety, producing bright orange fruits. The new bush variety 'Cream of the Crop' has white skin and pale flesh.

Pear-shaped butternut varieties are very versatile, and are excellent in soups or in any recipe calling for pumpkins. 'Butternut' has dark creamy-orange, club-shaped fruits with orange flesh; its fruits grow

large and keep well. The trailing 'Cobnut' is an early-ripening squash, with comparatively small, well-flavoured fruits. 'Sprinter' is an early-ripening form with smallish fruits.

ABOVE Little pattypan squashes have a firmer texture than courgettes (zucchini), but the flavour is similar.

BELOW The hybrid squash and golden acorn squash can be baked whole in their skins and served with butter.

ABOVE The delicate mottled surface pattern of the 'Fig Leaf' squash disguises a hard skin.

ABOVE The colours of acorn squashes range from green, through yellow to golden. The skin and flesh are soft.

ABOVE The delightful small 'Red Kuri', which is a type of Hubbard squash, has a hard flesh and a bright red colour.

Delicata varieties, which are usually pale yellow with succulent flesh, include 'Delicata', which bears small fruits with orange flesh and a sweet flavour, and 'Sweet Dumpling', which has round, green and cream fruits, with sweet, well-textured flesh.

Hubbard varieties are large winter squashes, which are best mashed or puréed. The original Hubbard squash is 'Green Hubbard' ('Hubbard', 'True Hubbard'), which has green fruits with tough skins and well-flavoured, rather dry flesh. The fruits, which can weigh up to 35kg/15lb, keep well in winter. 'Blue Ballet' is a smaller version of the well-known 'Blue Hubbard', which produces large, rectangular fruits that keep well. 'Golden Hubbard' has large orange fruits. 'Red Kuri', which is also sold as 'Onion Squash' and 'Uchiki Kuri', has onion-sized, bright red fruits with tasty flesh.

Buttercup or kabocha squashes usually have bright green skins and pale orange flesh. They are similar in both flavour and texture to acorn squashes and are prepared and eaten in the same way. They include 'Buttercup', which has medium-sized, dark green fruits, weighing up to 1.5kg/3lb 5oz, with bright orange, flavourful flesh.

'Black Forest' is an old-fashioned variety bearing small fruits and dark orange flesh. 'Delicata' has a creamy skin with green stripes, and the tasty, dark green fruits of 'Sweet Mama' are produced on short vines.

Pattypan squashes resemble small custard squashes. They can be pale green, yellow or white, and they have a rather firmer texture than courgettes, although the taste is similar. 'Peter Pan' has pale green, rather flattened fruits, which can be picked and cooked in the same way as courgettes. 'Sunburst' is a good-cropping variety with bright yellow fruits.

ABOVE The highly coloured 'Turk's Turban' squash has firm flesh.

ABOVE The 'Melonette St Julien' has a smooth, soft skin and the flesh is soft.

ABOVE 'Sweet Dumpling' has variegated green skin and sweet, orange flesh.

ABOVE Butternut squashes are pear-shaped and usually a soft yellow colour. The flesh is excellent in soups.

ABOVE The banana squash is soft and has an unusual elongated shape. It gives an elegant display when carved.

Squashes have a tough rind and central seeds and fibres that should be removed before cooking. Unless baking in the skin, peel squashes with a large, sturdy knife. Scrape away the seeds and stringy fibres.

Boil in a little water for about 20 minutes until tender, then mash and serve with butter and plenty of salt and pepper. Smaller squashes can be baked whole in their skins, then halved, seeded and served with butter and maple syrup. Larger squashes can also be lightly sautéed in butter before being mixed with stock, cream or chopped tomatoes.

Spaghetti squashes are long and pale yellow, and they can grow large. When they are cooked, the flesh resembles spaghetti. 'Tivoli' produces several medium to large fruits on a short vine. The fruits have crunchy white flesh, with a sweet flavour; this is a good choice if you want squash for stir fries and salads. The fruits of 'Stripetti' are boldly striped with green, and they have a spaghetti-like texture.

There are also a number of novelty squashes. 'Gold Nugget' bears small orange fruits on a bushy plant. 'Pink Banana' is an old North American variety, producing very long fruits (75cm/30in or more) that resemble pink bananas. The bright colours and odd shape (30cm/12in across) of 'Turk's Turban' make it highly decorative and unusual. The small fruit of 'Fancycrook' squashes have very curved, bright yellow necks and large, meaty bulbs.

NUTRITION

Squashes contain high amounts of vitamins A and E, beta carotene and potassium. Beta carotene and vitamin E are antioxidants and are believed to reduce the risk of certain cancers. Because of their high water content, all squashes are low in calories.

To stuff a squash, use a teaspoon to remove the insides, taking care not to cut the outer skin or base. Save the seeds to see if they will germinate for a new crop. Add a filling of your choice, for example cooked lamb and rice, butter, breadcrumbs, milk, onion, parsley, eggs and seasoning. Bake at 190°C/375°F/Gas 5 until tender, then sprinkle with feta cheese and basil.

ABOVE Spaghetti squashes should be cooked like vegetable marrows.

ABOVE Pattypan squashes have a flat, dish-like shape with pretty deckle edges.

Cucumbers *Cucumis sativus*

One of the quickest ways to prepare a meal is to pop into the garden, grab a lettuce, some tomatoes and a cucumber, add some fresh, crusty bread – and there you are. Most gardeners grow lettuces and tomatoes, but fewer grow cucumbers, perhaps because they think they require a greenhouse or they are more difficult to grow. Neither need be the case. Outdoor cucumbers can be grown as easily as courgettes (zucchini), which few gardeners find a problem.

cucumber

HISTORY

Cucumbers have been used as a vegetable for the best part of 5,000 years. They were first grown and eaten in India, where they were developed from a native species. From there they spread north-east into China and north-west into Greece and Rome.

There are several colours and shapes available. Westerners are more used to long cucumbers with green skins, but they can also be oval or even round, and colours can range from white to yellow.

As far as the gardener is concerned, there are two types of cucumber: the climbing varieties with long fruits that are grown under glass, and the ridge varieties, which are much shorter and are grown in the open. The advantage of greenhouse varieties is that they can be started earlier and are not as dependent on the weather. Ridge varieties, on the other hand, need less looking after and are less prone to attack by pests and diseases, which thrive in the warmth of the greenhouse. From the culinary point of view, the greenhouse forms are often preferred, mainly because outdoor cucumbers have tough, often prickly, skins and do not look quite as elegant as their indoor cousins. Until recently, many outdoor varieties tended to taste bitter, but selective breeding means that this is now no longer generally the case.

LEFT The small cucumbers known as Kirbys are usually pickled.

VARIETIES

Ridge
'Boothby's Blonde'
'Burpless Tasty Green'
'Bush Champion'
'Crystal Apple'
'Kyoto'
'Long Green Ridge'
'Long White'
'Masterpiece'
'Teide'
'Zeina'

Greenhouse
'Aidas'
'Birgit'
'Carmen'
'Fenumex'
'Flamingo'
'Pepinex'
'Petita'
'Telegraph'
'Telegraph Improved'

Gherkins
'Besta'
'Conda'
'Eureka'
'Venlo Pickling'

ABOVE In cool areas ridge cucumbers can be grown outdoors. New varieties do not taste bitter.

Gherkins are a form of ridge cucumber, which are used for pickling. Any immature ridge cucumber can be used, but some varieties have been specially bred for the purpose. Like courgettes and marrows, there is no difference in cultivation technique other than the time of picking.

VARIETIES

Cucumbers are usually classified as indoor or outdoor varieties. Most greenhouse or indoor cucumbers bear long, cylindrical fruits, usually dark green with smooth skins. Outdoor or ridge cucumbers can be grown outdoors in cool climates, as can gherkins.

In the greenhouse, the all-female cucumber 'Flamingo' produces a good crop of uniformly sized, dark green fruits, which are guaranteed not to taste bitter. It has some resistance to powdery mildew and to leaf mould (cladosporium). The vigorous 'Aidas' bears long, green fruits with an excellent flavour; it will grow in an unheated or slightly heated greenhouse and shows resistance to both scab and leaf spot. 'Carmen' shows above average resistance to diseases.

Some cucumbers will grow either under glass or in the open garden. The crisp, fairly short and fat fruits of the climbing or trailing 'Burpless Tasty Green' do not become bitter. They are at their best when they are no more than 25cm/10in long. The variety has some resistance to powdery mildew. 'Bush Champion' is a compact bush cucumber with dark green fruits. Said to be resistant to cucumber mosaic virus, it is a good choice for a large container. The vigorous 'Kyoto' produces plenty of well-flavoured, large fruits, 64cm/25in long and up to 4cm/1½in in diameter, with firm flesh. 'Teide', which shows good resistance to powdery mildew, has the advantage of remaining succulent and crisp for a long time after picking. 'Zeina', which has smooth-skinned fruit, has been developed to produce a heavy crop of mini-cucumbers.

'Crystal Apple' is a traditional, heavy-cropping variety for outdoors. It produces small, roundish, yellowish fruits on trailing stems. The fruits, which taste like ordinary cucumbers, are at their best eaten young. It can be grown in a large container or even a flower border, as long as it is provided with support.

Cucumbers are not always green. 'Long White', a strongly growing form suitable for outdoors or indoors, has thin, tender, white skin and juicy, tasty flesh. 'Boothby's Blonde' is an old variety from the USA. The fruits get to 15–20cm/6–8in long and have rather blunt ends. The skin is yellowish, with small black spines, and the flesh is sweet and succulent.

Finally, if you like gherkins, look out for 'Eureka', which shows good disease resistance and bears a heavy crop of evenly sized fruits. 'Conda' and 'Venlo Pickling' produce rather short gherkins on trailing plants.

NUTRITION

Cucumbers contain a lot of water and hardly any fat or carbohydrate, making them low in calories, and also reasonable amounts of vitamin C and some carotene. In addition, they have some potassium, vitamin A and vitamin B complex.

PREPARING

Whether you peel a cucumber or not is a matter of personal preference, but wash it if you don't intend to peel it. Home-grown cucumbers don't have the wax coatings that commercial producers add, so they shouldn't need peeling. Special citrus peelers can remove strips of peel to give an attractive striped effect. To remove the seeds, cut the cucumber in half lengthways and scoop out the seeds with a teaspoon.

planning and
preparation

Whether you are growing crops in a
greenhouse or in the open garden, it is
essential to provide them with the best
conditions you can. Fertile, well-drained,
moisture-retentive soil will get your plants off
to the best possible start. Help your plants to
thrive by feeding and watering them regularly.
Keep an eye out for pests and diseases and
take appropriate action promptly. Your plants
will reward you with prolific, healthy harvests.

Types of soil

Courgettes (zucchini), marrows, pumpkins, squashes and cucumbers can be grown in most types of ground, although they tend to be greedy feeders, so it is important to make sure that the soil is not only well-drained and moisture-retentive but also fertile. It is especially important that the soil does not dry out, because all these plants need plenty of moisture when they are fruiting so they are not checked. Maintaining the soil in good condition will quickly become a routine once you have determined the type of soil that you have in your garden. There are now simple and inexpensive kits that quickly show both the pH and the level of nutrients in garden soil so that you can provide the perfect conditions for your chosen crops.

CLAY SOIL

This type of soil can be difficult and heavy to work, and the particles cling together, making the soil sticky. Clay soil compacts easily, forming solid lumps that roots find hard to penetrate and making it difficult to dig. Try not to walk on clay soil when it is wet, which will compact the soil even more. In addition, clay soil is slow to drain in wet weather, but, when it is dry, it can set like concrete. It can also be cold and slow to warm up in spring, making it unsuitable for early crops. On the other hand, clay soil is slow to cool down in autumn, and it can be easily improved by the addition of well-rotted compost or manure and made easier to handle by the incorporation of grit. It is usually rich, and the hard work involved in the initial stages of improving it will pay off in the long term.

SANDY SOIL

Soils made up of sand and silts are composed of individual grains that allow water to pass through them quickly, and this speedy passage of water through the soil tends to leach (wash) out nutrients. Sandy soils are often rather poor and do not retain moisture well. However, they can be quick to warm up in spring, making them ideal for early crops. Silty soil contains particles that are more clay-like in texture than those found in sandy soils, and they hold more moisture and nutrients. Both types of soil are easy to improve and are not difficult to work. Sand does not compact as clay does, although it is still not good practice to walk on beds, but silty soil is susceptible to the impact of feet. Adding well-rotted organic material will make both types more moisture-retentive.

LOAM

This type of soil is a combination of clay and sandy soils, with the best characteristics of both. It tends to be both free-draining and also moisture-retentive. Although this may seem to be a contradiction in terms, it means that the soil is sufficiently free draining to allow excess water to drain away easily, but some is retained, so that both water and air are available to the plants' roots, enabling them to take up the nutrients they need. Loamy soil is the ideal for which gardeners strive.

ACID AND ALKALINE SOILS

Soils are also sometimes classified by their acidity or alkalinity. Those that are based on peat (peat moss) are acid; those that include chalk or limestone are alkaline. A scale of pH levels is used to indicate the

WORKING IN ORGANIC MATTER

1 Soil that has been dug in the autumn can have more organic matter worked into the top layer in the spring. Spread the organic matter over the surface.

2 Lightly work the organic material into the top layer of soil with a fork. There is no need for full-scale digging because worms will take the humus down.

1 Collect the soil sample 5–8cm/2–3in below the surface. Take a number of samples, but test each one separately.

2 With this kit, mix one part of soil with five parts of water. Shake well in a jar, then allow the water to settle.

3 Draw off some of the settled liquid from the top few centimetres (about an inch) for your test.

4 Carefully transfer the solution to the test chamber in the plastic container, using the pipette.

5 Select a colour-coded capsule (one for each nutrient). Put the powder in the chamber, replace the cap and shake.

6 After a few minutes, compare the colour of the liquid with the shade panel of the container.

degree of acidity or alkalinity. Neutral soil has a pH of 7; a pH lower than that indicates acidity, while a pH above 7 indicates an alkaline soil. Use one of the simple testing kits to check the soil in your garden. Take samples from several places about 8cm/3in down and follow the manufacturer's instructions.

SOIL FOR CONTAINERS

Plants grown under glass are usually in containers of some kind, and there is a much smaller amount of growing medium available to plants in containers than is available to those in the open garden, where their roots can range freely in search of moisture and nutrients. It is important, therefore, that an especially fertile growing medium is used from the start for container-grown plants. Many gardeners like the convenience of ready-packed growing bags, which contain sufficient compost (soil mix) for two or, at most, three plants, provided you feed and water them regularly throughout the growing season. After harvesting the crops, the contents of the growing bag should either be spread as a mulch at the back of the ornamental border or added to the compost heap. Do not try to grow anything else in it because it will contain no nutrients.

In the past, gardeners would have their own preferred recipes for growing different plants, mixing different proportions of loam, leaf mould and well-rotted manure with fertilizers. Most gardeners today choose the simpler option of buying ready-mixed compost. Avoid those based on peat (peat moss), because of the environmental damage caused by collecting it.

Improving the soil

Once you have established the type of soil in your garden, perhaps the most important task in the garden is to improve and maintain the quality of the soil. Good-quality soil is the aim of any gardener who wants to grow a range of vegetables, and to ignore the quality of the soil is to ignore one of a garden's greatest assets and will lead to poor yields and plants that are susceptible to pests and diseases.

IMPROVING SOIL QUALITY

The key to improving the soil in your garden is well-rotted organic material, especially garden compost, made from garden waste and vegetable waste from the kitchen, and farmyard manure. Both compost and manure are invaluable for improving the texture of the soil, and also contain significant amounts of nutrients.

It is important that such material is well rotted. If it is still in the process of rotting down when it is applied to the soil it will extract nitrogen from the soil as it continues to break down. This is, of course, the opposite of what the gardener wants – the aim is to add nitrogen to the soil. A good indicator that the material has broken down is that it is odourless. Even horse manure is free from odour once it has rotted down. Some bought-in materials contain undesirable chemicals, but these will be removed if the material is stacked and allowed to weather. Bark and other shredded woody materials may contain resins, for example, while animal and bird manures may contain ammonia from urea. These chemicals will evaporate or be converted during the weathering process.

Although some crops should not be grown on recently manured ground – it causes root vegetables to fork – courgettes (zucchini) and marrows, and squashes and pumpkins are greedy plants, which will thrive if they are planted in soil that contains plenty of well-rotted compost or manure.

DIGGING IN

When vegetables are grown in a dedicated part of the garden, the best way to apply organic material is to dig it in so that it is incorporated into the soil. If possible, double dig the bed, adding organic material all the way to the bottom of both spits. This will help the soil to conserve moisture and supply nutrients where they are needed, which is down around the roots. It will also encourage the roots to delve deeply, so that the plants are well anchored in the soil, rather than remaining on the surface where easy water can be obtained from rainfall and the watering can. The deeper the roots go, the more consistent will be the plant's water supply, and the plant will grow at a regular pace rather than in unproductive fits and starts. This will produce better plants and well-shaped fruits.

TOP-DRESSING

Once the ground has been planted, it is best not to dig around the plants, since this is likely to damage their roots. Organic matter

IMPROVING SOIL FERTILITY

The fertility of the soil is much improved by the addition of organic material, but a quick boost can also be achieved by adding an organic fertilizer, spreading it over the surface and then raking it in.

REDUCING SOIL ACIDITY

The acidity of the soil can be reduced by adding lime some weeks before planting and working it in with a rake. Check the soil with a soil testing kit to see how much lime is required.

can still be added, however, simply by spreading it on the surface of the soil around the plants. A layer 10cm/4in deep will be slowly worked into the soil by earthworms and other soil dwellers, and the dressing will also act as a mulch, protecting the ground from drying out as well as preventing weed seeds from germinating. Make sure that the top-dressing is free from weed seeds, or this last benefit will be lost, but hoeing off any weeds as they appear should not be too difficult. When garden soil has been thoroughly dug and plenty of organic matter added at the depth of one or two spades, many gardeners prefer not to dig the soil again. Instead, they apply a deep annual mulch. Applying a loose mulch such as chipped bark or cocoa shells will help to keep down weeds and conserve moisture in the ground.

WORKING ON WET SOIL

It is best to avoid working on wet soil, but sometimes it is necessary. To ensure that the soil is not compacted and its structure destroyed, it is advisable to work from a plank of wood.

IMPROVING SOIL STRUCTURE

1 One of the best ways to improve the structure of the soil is to add as much organic material as you can, preferably when the soil is dug. For heavy soils, this is best done in the autumn.

2 If the soil has already been dug, well-rotted organic material can be worked into the surface of the soil with a fork. The worms will complete the task of working it into the soil.

AMENDING THE SOIL'S PH

Courgettes, marrows, squashes and pumpkins prefer soil with a pH of 5.5–6.8; cucumbers will tolerate more neutral soil, from 5.5 to 7.0. If you find that your soil has a pH below 5.5, which indicates acid conditions, you can adjust the pH upwards by adding lime to the soil. Ordinary lime (calcium carbonate) is the safest form to use. Quicklime (calcium oxide) is the strongest and most caustic, but it may cause damage and must be used with great care. Slaked lime (calcium hydroxide), which is quicklime with water added, is not as strong as quicklime and is easier to handle. Choose a windless day, wear protective clothing and follow the supplier's instructions about quantities to the letter. Do not try to overcompensate for an acid soil by adding more lime than is recommended as this may lead to nutrient deficiency. Do not add lime at the same time as manure because this will release ammonia, which can damage plants. Do not sow or plant in the ground for at least a month after liming the soil. Mushroom compost, which is rich in lime, can be used instead.

It is more difficult to reduce the pH levels of alkaline soils. The traditional method was digging in peat (peat moss), but not only does it break down quickly and need to be continually replaced, the collection of peat is now regarded as environmentally unacceptable. In any case, most soils tend to be slightly acid because calcium is continually leached out by rainfall, and most organic manures tend to be slightly acid and will help to reduce pH levels. Leaf mould, especially when it is made from pine needles, is also acid. If the soil in your garden is too alkaline for cultivating these vegetables, consider using raised beds, which you can fill with topsoil bought in from elsewhere.

Compost

This is a valuable material for any garden, but it is especially useful in the fruit and vegetable garden. It is free, apart from any capital required in installing compost bins, and these should last for many years, so the overall cost should be negligible. A little effort is required, but this is a small price to pay for the resulting gold dust.

THE PRINCIPLE

In making compost, gardeners emulate the natural process in which a plant takes nutrients from the soil, dies and then rots, so the nutrients return to the ground. In the garden, waste plant material is collected, piled in a heap and allowed to rot down before being returned to the soil as crumbly, sweet-smelling, fibrous material.

Because it is kept in a heap, the rotting material generates heat, which encourages it to break down more quickly. The heat also helps to kill pests and diseases, as well as any weed seed in the compost. The balance of air and moisture is important; if the heap is too wet it will go slimy, but if it is too dry it will not decompose. The best balance is achieved by having some ventilation, but protecting the compost from rain, and by using a good mixture of materials.

RIGHT Good compost is dark brown, crumbly and has a sweet, earthy smell, not a rotting one.

The process should take up to about three months, but many old-fashioned gardeners like to retain the heap for much longer than that, growing marrows and courgettes (zucchini) in a layer of soil on top before they break it up for use in the garden.

THE COMPOST BIN

Gardeners always seem to generate more garden waste than they ever thought possible and never to have enough compost space, so when planning your bins, make sure you have enough. The ideal aim is to have three: one to hold new waste, one that is in the process of breaking down, and a third that is ready for use.

Bins are traditionally made from wood (often scrap wood), and because these can be hand-made to fit your space and the amount of material available, this is still the best option. Sheet materials, such as corrugated iron, can also be

ABOVE A range of organic materials can be used, but avoid cooked kitchen waste or any weeds that have seed in them. Clockwise from top left: kitchen waste, weeds, shreddings and grass clippings.

used. Most ready-made bins are made of reinforced black or green plastic, and although these work perfectly well, they may be a bit on the small side in a busy garden.

You can make compost in a bin the size of a dustbin (trash can), but if you have room, one holding a cubic metre/35 cubic feet, or even bigger, will be much more efficient.

The simplest bin can be made by nailing together four wooden pallets to form a box. If the front is made so that the slats are slotted in to form the wall, they can be removed as the bin is emptied, making the job of removing the compost easier.

MATERIALS

Most garden plant waste can be used for composting, but do not include perennial weeds. Weed seeds will be killed if the compost heats up really well, but it is safest not to include them. You could have a separate bin for anything that contains seeds because the compost can then be used for permanent plantings such as trees. If the compost never comes to the surface, seeds will not germinate. Woody material, such as hedge clippings, can be used, but shred it first. Kitchen vegetable waste, such as peelings and cores, can be used, but avoid cooked vegetables and do not include meat, which will attract rats and other vermin.

TECHNIQUE

Placing a few branches or twiggy material in the bottom of the bin will help to keep the contents aerated. Put in the material as it becomes available, but avoid building up deep layers of any one material, especially grass cuttings. Mix them with other materials.

To help keep the heap warm, cover it with an old carpet or sheet of plastic. This also prevents rainwater from chilling the contents and swamping the air spaces. The lid should be kept on until the compost is needed.

Every so often, add a layer of farmyard manure if you can get it, because it will provide extra nitrogen to speed things up. Failing this, you can buy special compost accelerators. It is not essential to add manure or an accelerator, however – it just means waiting a couple of months longer.

Air is important, and this usually percolates through the side of the bin, so leave a few gaps between the timbers. If you use old pallets, these are usually crudely made, with plenty of gaps. The colder material around the edges takes longer to break down, so turn the compost around every so often. This also loosens the pile and allows air to circulate.

MAKING COMPOST

1 To make garden compost, place a layer of "browns" – straw, dry leaves and chipped wood are ideal – into the bin, to a depth of about 15cm/6in.

2 Begin a layer of "greens" – any green plant material, except perennial or seeding weeds. Fibrous or woody stems should be cut up small or shredded.

3 Add greens until you have a layer 15cm/6in thick. Mix lawn clippings with other green waste to avoid the layer becoming slimy and airless.

4 Kitchen refuse, including fruit and vegetable waste and eggshells, can be added, but not cooked or fatty foods. Cover the heap.

5 Turn the heap occasionally. The speed of composting will vary, but when ready, the compost should be brown, crumbly and sweet-smelling.

Soil fertility

You cannot go on taking things out of the soil without putting anything back. In nature plants return the nutrients they have taken from the soil when they die. In the garden the vegetables are removed, and the chain is broken. Compost and other organic materials help to redress the balance, but to grow high-yielding crops, fertilizers may be needed as well.

WHAT PLANTS REQUIRE

The main foods required by plants are nitrogen (N), phosphorus (P) and potassium (K), with smaller quantities of magnesium (Mg), calcium (Ca) and sulphur (S). They also require small amounts of what are known as trace elements, including iron (Fe) and manganese (Mn).

Each of the main nutrients tends to be used by the plant for one specific function. Thus nitrogen is concerned with plant growth and is used for promoting the rapid growth of the green parts of the plant. Phosphorus, usually in the form of phosphates, is used to create good root growth as well as

RIGHT To add nutrients naturally to the soil, rot down old plant material in a compost bin, and then return it to the soil.

helping with the ripening of fruits, while potassium, in the form of potash, is used to promote flowering and formation of good fruit.

THE NATURAL WAY

The most natural way to add nutrients to the soil is to use compost and other organic matter. Such materials are important to the general structure of the soil, but they also feed it. Well-rotted farmyard manure and garden compost have been the main way that gardeners have traditionally fed their gardens. However, some gardeners, especially those in towns, may not have easy access to large quantities of these organic materials, or space to store them. Bought fertilizers, either organic or inorganic, can be a simple way of giving plants the nutrients they need.

Organic materials normally contains less of the main nutrients than concentrated fertilizers, but they are often strong in trace elements, and although they may not contain such a strong

ORGANIC FERTILIZERS

blood

bonemeal

seaweed meal

fish/blood/bone

concentration of nitrogen, they do release it over a longer period which is of great benefit. Because of their other benefits, farmyard manure and garden compost are still the best way of treating the soil and for improving its texture.

ORGANIC FERTILIZERS

Concentrated fertilizers can be either organic or inorganic. Organic fertilizers are made from naturally occurring organic materials. Bonemeal (ground-up bones) is quite strong in nitrogen and phosphates, making it a good fertilizer to promote growth, especially at the start of a plant's life. Bonemeal also has the advantage that it breaks down slowly, releasing the fertilizer over a long period. When you apply bonemeal, you may want to wear gloves. Other organic fertilizers include fish, blood and bone (containing quick-release nitrogen and also phosphorous); hoof and horn (high in nitrogen); and seaweed meal (containing nitrogen and potassium).

Because they are purely natural products, they are used by organic growers.

INORGANIC FERTILIZERS

These are fertilizers that have been made artificially, although they are frequently derived from natural rocks and minerals and the process may just involve crushing. They are concentrated and are usually soluble in water. This means that they are instantly available for plants and are useful for giving a plant a push when it is required.

Growmore (not available in USA)

sulphate of ammonia

potash

superphosphate

They do tend to wash out of the soil and need to be replaced. Some are general fertilizers, with equal proportions of nitrogen, phosphorus and potassium. Others are much more specific. Superphosphate, for example, is entirely used for supplying phosphorus; potash (potassium sulphate) provides potassium; and ammonium nitrate is added when nitrogen is required.

Increasing numbers of gardeners are turning against inorganic fertilizers, unaware that they may not be as artificial as is generally believed. Many are not classified as organic simply because they are not derived from living things. Nevertheless, it is their concentrated form and the fact that they can be readily washed from the soil that leads many gardeners to object.

SLOW-RELEASE FERTILIZERS

A modern trend is to coat fertilizers so they are released slowly into the soil. These are expensive in the short term, but because they do not leach away and do not need to be replaced as frequently, they save trouble and ensure a regular nutrient supply. They are particularly useful for container planting, where constant watering is necessary (with its attendant rapid nutrient leaching).

Digging the soil

Although it is a technique that is now being questioned by some gardeners, digging is still one of the main garden activities. It breaks up the soil, allowing the ingress of water and air, which are both important for plant growth. In addition, it also allows organic material to be incorporated deep down in the soil, right where the roots need it.

Digging enables you to remove weed roots – especially important on previously uncultivated ground – and it also helps bring pests to the surface, where many will die or be eaten by birds or other predators.

SINGLE DIGGING

The most frequently carried out method is single digging, and there are two ways, one informal and the other formal. The informal method is best used when the ground is quite loose; the gardener simply forks it over, turning it and replacing it in the same position, hardly using any trench at all. This process is often carried out on light or sandy soils.

SINGLE DIGGING

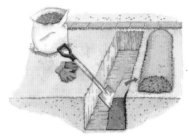

1 Start by digging a trench to one spade's depth across the plot, putting the soil from the first trench to one side to be used later in the final trench.

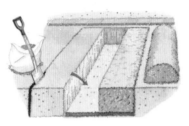

3 Repeat this process of adding manure to each trench and filling in with earth from the next, breaking up the soil as you go and keeping the surface even.

2 Put a layer of manure in the bottom of the trench. Dig out the next trench and cover the manure with earth taken from the second trench.

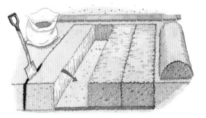

4 Continue down the length of the plot until you reach the final trench. This should be filled in with the earth taken from the first trench.

Formal single digging is necessary on heavier soils and when there is organic material to be incorporated. First, a trench is dug across the width of the plot, and the earth from the trench is taken to the other end of the bed. Compost or farmyard manure is put into the bottom of the trench and then another trench is dug. The earth removed from the trench is

LEFT After a winter exposed to the weather, most soils can be broken down into a fine tilth by using a rake. More recently turned soil may need to be broken down with a heavier hoe first.

put into the first trench to cover the organic material. This procedure is repeated down the length of the plot. When the final trench has been dug and organic material placed in it, it is refilled with the soil taken from the first trench.

Alternatively, the first trench can be dug so that it is two trenches wide. Organic material is put in the bottom as usual, and then the next trench is dug but the soil is spread over the bottom of the previous two trenches, only half-filling them. This is then covered with more organic material and then the fourth trench dug, filling up the first. Trenches three and four are treated in the same way, being filled first with the soil from trench five and then that from trench six.

DOUBLE DIGGING

Double digging is employed to break up the subsoil and is useful on any new plot of ground as well as when deep beds are being prepared. Dig the trench as before, taking the earth to the end of the plot. Dig the subsoil in the bottom of the trench to the depth of a fork or spade, adding in organic material. Add more organic material on top and then dig the next trench, placing the soil into the

RIGHT For larger gardens with heavy soil, a rotavator (rototiller) will break down the soil into a fine tilth. Even a small one saves a lot of time, especially if the soil is too dry to break down with a rake.

first. Repeat until the end of the plot is reached. Do not bring any subsoil up to the top.

MECHANICAL DIGGING

A mechanical rotavator (rototiller) can save time and effort on a large plot. One disadvantage is that it cuts up weed roots into small pieces, making them more difficult to remove by hand than with conventional digging.

BREAKING DOWN INTO A FINE TILTH FOR SOWING

The best time to dig a heavy soil is in the autumn, then the winter frosts and rain will break it down for you. If clay soils are dug in the spring and allowed to dry out too much, they are difficult to break down because the clods set like concrete. A mechanical rotavator makes breaking the soil down easier. Work on the soil when it is neither waterlogged nor completely dry, breaking it down, first with a large hoe and then with a rake. Shuffling along the surface with your feet will also help considerably, but do not do this if the ground is wet.

It is better to leave sandy soils until the spring because they do not need much breaking down. Raking the surface is usually all that is required.

Occasionally, the soil becomes too hard to break down. If this happens, water the soil with a sprinkler, leave it to dry slightly – so that it is no longer muddy – and then break it down. Alternatively, draw out a deep sowing row in the rough soil, fill it with potting compost (soil mix) and sow in this.

DOUBLE DIGGING

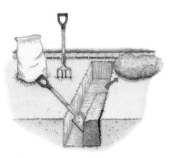

1 Dig a trench to one spade's depth, placing the soil to one side to be used later when filling in the final trench.

2 Break up the soil at the bottom of the trench, adding manure to the soil as you proceed.

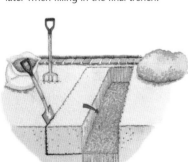

3 Dig the next trench, turning the soil over on top of the broken soil in the first trench.

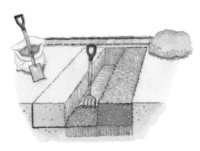

4 Continue down the plot, ensuring that subsoil from the bottom of the trenches is not mixed with topsoil.

Weather problems

Gardeners are always at the mercy of the weather, and unpredictable weather can wreak havoc with vegetable crops. However, with forethought, many potential problems can be averted.

WIND

If your garden is exposed, most vegetables will need some protection from wind, and squashes, with their large, soft leaves, are especially vulnerable. The best windbreak is a hedge. Unlike a wall, which causes turbulence as the wind passes over it, a hedge will allow some air to pass through, thus avoiding turbulence while greatly reducing the wind's speed. Hedges take time to grow, however, and a good alternative, though less attractive, is special plastic netting; make sure it is supported by strong, firmly anchored posts.

FROST

Squashes and pumpkins are among the more tender vegetables, and large varieties in particular need a long growing season in order to ripen well. With the smaller fruits such as courgettes (zucchini), a longer season means that crops can be harvested over a longer period. In cool climates, therefore, these plants are always best started off under glass, so that they can be planted out as soon as the danger of frosts has passed.

As well as paying close attention to weather forecasts, it is important to consider the situation of the vegetable plot. Shelter, and warm house walls, can make a great difference to temperatures, and it is a good idea to test different parts of the garden with a maximum/minimum thermometer. If your garden is in a frost pocket, where cold air sinks and becomes trapped, it may be possible to make a hole in the hedge or fence at the lowest point, enabling air to flow through. Alternatively, a hedge higher up the slope could deflect the cold air as it moves downhill.

There are a number of forms of frost protection, and these generally have two main uses: they can be placed over the ground in early spring, to allow the soil to warm up more quickly before planting out; and they can be used to cover plants temporarily when frost is expected. Cloches, made of glass or plastic, are available either as long tunnels or domes for individual plants; they can also be improvised using cut-off plastic bottles. Individual cloches have the added advantage of protecting against slugs. Horticultural fleece is a light, woven fabric that can be placed over plants; like cloches, it allows light through, so can be left on during the day. Black plastic is effective, whether plain or the horticultural version which allows air and water to penetrate, but cannot be left over plants during the day. Newspaper can also provide good insulation, if you drop several layers from a height to create air pockets; this also excludes light. Another effective insulator is straw, but in windy

LEFT If a hedge creates a frost pocket, cut a hole in the base so that the air can flow through.

Most automatic watering systems have a control system to reduce the water pressure, and some also act as a filter.

Drip-feed systems can be used for beds and containers. T-joints allow tubes to be attached for individual drip heads.

A timing device can be preset to turn water on and off automatically, if you are away from home for a while.

weather it will need anchoring with a box or sheets of plastic weighted down with stones.

DROUGHT

Plenty of water is crucial for most vegetables, and this is especially true of squashes and pumpkins; if they do not receive a constant and abundant supply, their growth will be checked and the fruits will not develop properly. Incorporating plenty of organic material into the soil will improve the texture, helping it to hold moisture, and this is especially important for light, sandy soils. It has the added advantage of providing nutrients, which are also needed in large quantities by these crops. Covering the ground with a mulch, either of organic material or black plastic, will greatly reduce water loss through evaporation. Obviously, it should not be applied when the soil is dry, as it will prevent rain from entering.

When all these precautions have been taken, however, the plants are still likely to need

watering over the summer. Whatever method of watering you use, remember that "little and often" can do more harm than good: it wets the surface, encouraging plants to form shallow roots, so they are less able to tap into deeper water reserves in the soil. A thorough soaking, at longer intervals, is much more beneficial.

Watering cans are a good way of making sure the water is directed where it is needed, but the task can be laborious if you have a large number of plants. A hand-held hose makes the job easier. Automatic systems reduce the work even more, but can be wasteful; a sprinkler will be hard to confine to the area where water is needed, and will also waste a lot through evaporation. A dribble hose is much more effective; it is laid on the ground and allows water to seep out slowly through tiny holes. If the ground is

mulched, place it under the mulch. It can even be buried in the soil and left in place permanently.

Automatic systems can be connected to a timer, which may be useful if you go away, or even if you are out during the day. Remember that it is best to water in the evening if possible, to reduce evaporation in the sun; wetting plants in hot sunshine can also cause scorching of the leaves.

RIGHT A maximum/minimum thermometer is useful for checking temperatures, both in the open garden and in the greenhouse.

Pests and diseases

The list of potential pests and diseases that can affect squashes can so alarm gardeners that they decide not to try growing these vegetables at all. This is a shame, because as long as the ground around them is kept well weeded and well fertilized, the healthy, vigorous plants will be able to fend off most problems. For some gardeners one of the most difficult aspects of controlling problems is to be completely ruthless about digging up and disposing of diseased crops – they should be thrown away or burned, not composted. It is far better to have a gap in the garden for a few months than to allow a disease or pest to become endemic.

BELOW Sticky traps are a form of organic control that is becoming popular for a wide range of pests. Here, pheromones attract insect pests to the trap, where they get stuck. Other sticky traps consist of sheets of yellow plastic covered with a non-drying glue. These are mainly used in greenhouses.

A MIXED GARDEN

One of the best ways to reduce pest and disease attacks is to grow a wide range of crops, mixed together. This means that any problem which only affects one type of plant will have less opportunity to become established.

Growing plenty of flowers, especially open, daisy-like ones such as marigolds (all types) and poached-egg plants (*Limnanthes douglasii*), will attract many beneficial insects such as hoverflies, which will help to reduce the population of aphids. Many gardeners grow such flowers alongside vegetables in the kitchen garden, which brightens up the area as well as serving a useful purpose. Growing a selection of flowering herbs, such as thyme, rosemary and marjoram, will also attract a wide range of insects. Alternatively, since most squashes are attractive plants, you may wish to grow them amongst the flowers in the ornamental garden.

INSECT PESTS

When plants are grown under glass, the two most serious problems are red spider mite and whitefly. Red spider mite is often first noticed when the upper surface of the leaves is covered with small specks. If the infestation is unchecked, a fine white webbing will be seen and leaves will turn yellow and die. Mist regularly to encourage a damp atmosphere and introduce the predatory mite *Phytoseiulus persimilis*. Overuse of pesticides has led to resistance, and chemical sprays can damage cucumber fruits.

Minute glasshouse whitefly can be seen on the undersides of leaves. The larvae suck sap and produce honeydew. Pyrethrum sprays should be repeated every three days to bring the pest under control. A biological control, the wasp *Encarsia formosa*, is available and can be used when the temperature is about 18°C/64°F. Do not spray against other insect pests after a biological control has been introduced to the greenhouse.

Aphids (blackfly, greenfly and many other colours) suck the sap of plants, weakening them, checking the growth and often transmitting viral diseases. They also excrete sticky honeydew, which drops on to leaves below, providing a good environment for fungal moulds to develop. Bacterial infections can enter plants through the tiny holes made by the aphids' mouthparts. If you wish to use

chemicals, choose a selective insecticide, such as one containing pirimicarb, which will kill the aphids but not other, beneficial insects. Organic insecticides include pyrethrum, derris and insecticidal soaps. The larvae of a species of gall midge, *Aphidoletes aphidomyza*, feed on aphids and can be introduced as a biological control in the greenhouse. Outdoors, encourage natural predators, such as ladybirds (ladybugs), hoverflies and insectivorous birds. Remove small colonies with jets of water.

SLUGS AND SNAILS

Most of the damage done to vegetables of all kinds in the garden is caused by slugs and snails, which will eat their way

LEFT Slugs and snails have few friends among gardeners. They make holes in just about any part of a plant, often leaving it useless or even dead.

through above-ground parts of plants, often demolishing entire young plants.

Slugs, though not snails, can be killed using a biological control (nematodes), which can be watered into the soil in late summer. At night go out and collect all the slugs and snails you can see, putting them in a bucket of water so that you can dispose of them. Dishes of beer and upturned grapefruit skins can also be used to attract slugs, and some gardeners like to leave surplus seedlings near the vegetable plot so that slugs and snails will be attracted to the waste rather than to the crops themselves.

Chemical controls are available, but best avoided, since birds can be poisoned by eating the dead slugs.

DISEASES

The most serious disease to affect cucurbits is mosaic virus, sometimes known as cucumber mosaic virus, and it disfigures both

plants and flowers, causing the leaves to become puckered and mottled and, if unchecked, making the fruits inedible. The virus is generally carried into the garden by aphids, and good hygiene is essential, especially after handling infected plants, which should be destroyed. Where possible, buy certified virus-free plants.

Powdery mildew can be a problem in hot dry weather, when plants are under stress, and it is especially prevalent when plants are too close together. Space plants well so that air can circulate freely around them. The mildew causes a white, powdery coating on the leaves and stems of plants, especially courgettes (zucchini), when they are allowed to become dry at the roots. Increase watering and, as a last resort, spray with a systemic fungicide such as carbendazim. Remove and destroy all infected debris so that the virus cannot overwinter in the garden. Look for disease-resistant varieties.

Cucumbers are prone to fungal stem rot. Cut out and destroy any diseased tissue as soon you see it, and spray with carbendazim.

ABOVE Withered cucumbers can be the result of a simple lack of water, rather than any pest or disease.

ABOVE Powdery mildew affects plants, such as this courgette (zucchini), that are dry and too close together.

ABOVE Whitefly are a serious pest in a greenhouse. A biological control can be very effective in controlling their damage.

Tools and equipment

To look in the average garden centre you would imagine that you need a tremendous battery of tools and equipment before you could ever consider gardening, but in fact you can start (and continue) gardening with relatively few tools and no equipment at all.

Tools are personal things, so one gardener may always use a spade for digging, no matter how soft the ground, whereas another would always use a fork as long as the ground was not too heavy. The type of hoe for certain jobs is another subject on which gardeners hold widely different opinions.

BUYING TOOLS

It is not necessary to buy a vast armoury of tools when you first start gardening. Most jobs can be done with a small basic kit. When you are buying, always choose the best you can afford. Many of the cheaper tools are made of pressed steel, which soon becomes blunt, will often bend and may even break. Stainless steel is undoubtedly the best, but tools made of this tend to be expensive. Ordinary steel implements can be almost as good, especially if you keep them clean. Avoid tools that are made of aluminium. Trowels and hand forks especially are often made of aluminium, but they wear down and blunt quickly and are not good value for money.

SECOND-HAND

A good way to acquire a collection of tools is to buy them second-hand. As well as usually being cheaper than new ones, they are often made of much better steel than cheap, modern ones and still retain a keen edge, even after many years' use. Another potential advantage is that, in the past, gardening tools were made with a much greater variation in design and size. If you go to buy a modern spade, for example, you will probably find that the sizes in the shop are all the same – designed for the "average" gardener. Old tools come in all shapes and sizes, and if you find modern tools uncomfortable to use you are more likely to find an old one that is made just for you.

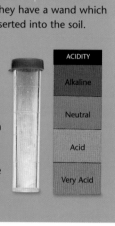

ACIDITY

Alkaline

Neutral

Acid

Very Acid

soil test meter

spade

fork

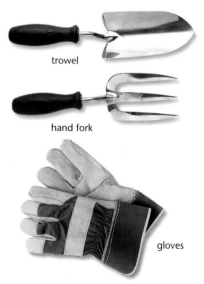

trowel

hand fork

gloves

Not all old tools are good by any means, of course, but by keeping an eye out and buying only good-quality ones you will end up with tools that will more than see you through your gardening career and at a relatively modest price. Look out for them at car boot sales (garage sales) and in rural junk shops (second-hand stores). Avoid antique shops where such tools are sold at inflated prices to be hung as decorations on the wall rather than to be used.

CARE AND MAINTENANCE

Look after your tools. If you do this they will not only always be in tip-top working condition but should last a lifetime. Scrape all the mud and any vegetation off the tools as soon as you have used them. Once they are clean, run an oily rag lightly over the metal parts. The thin film of oil will stop the metal from corroding. This not only makes the tools last longer but also makes them easier to use because less effort is needed to use a clean spade than one with a rough surface of rust.

In addition, keep the wooden parts of all tools clean, wiping them over with linseed oil if the wood becomes too dry.

Keep all blades sharp. Hang tools up if possible. Standing spades and hoes on the ground, especially if it is concrete, will blunt them over time. Keep them away from children.

EQUIPMENT

It is possible to run a vegetable garden with no mechanical aids at all. However, if you have grass paths, a lawn mower will, obviously, be more than useful – it will be essential. Hedge cutters, too, are useful, although hedges can be cut by hand much more easily than grass paths.

In the vegetable garden itself the only mechanical device that you may require is a rotavator (rototiller), which can be used for digging and breaking up the soil. This is far from essential, even in a large garden – after all, many gardeners enjoy digging – but it does make life easier if you want to break down a large area of heavy soil into a fine tilth.

Keep all your equipment maintained and serviced regularly, and always make sure you follow the manufacturer's safety instructions.

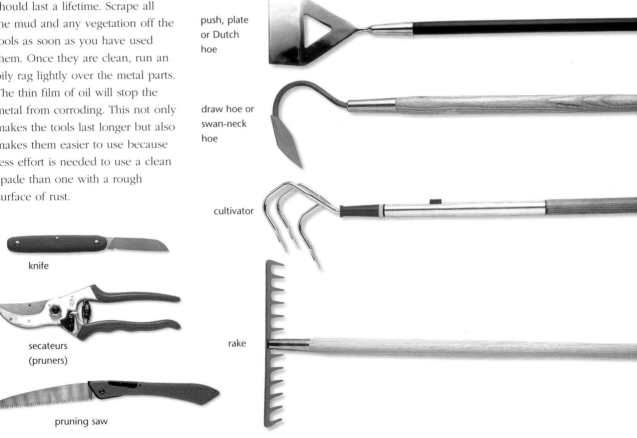

knife

secateurs
(pruners)

pruning saw

push, plate
or Dutch
hoe

draw hoe or
swan-neck
hoe

cultivator

rake

cultivating
squashes and pumpkins

Growing marrows and courgettes (zucchini), squashes, pumpkins and cucumbers is not difficult, and even first-time growers should be able to produce impressive crops from summer into late autumn with just a little bit of effort. In the garden they need moist, fertile, well-drained soil and plenty of sun. In the greenhouse they need regular watering and feeding, and if you are interested in growing some of the more unusual cultivars, you can easily raise your own plants from seed.

Growing in the vegetable plot

If your garden is small, you may not wish to have a separate plot for vegetables. A number of the more attractive types, including tomatoes and decorative salad leaves, can be successfully integrated into an ornamental garden. Most types of squashes are also attractive enough to be grown this way, but they do tend to take up a lot of space. If you grow only a few plants, they can look stunning in flower beds, or you could even grow them in tubs on a sunny patio. For growing larger quantities, however, it is usually best to have a dedicated vegetable garden.

DESIGNING THE BEDS

The positioning of a vegetable plot is an important consideration in the overall design of a garden.

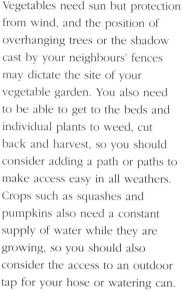

Vegetables need sun but protection from wind, and the position of overhanging trees or the shadow cast by your neighbours' fences may dictate the site of your vegetable garden. You also need to be able to get to the beds and individual plants to weed, cut back and harvest, so you should consider adding a path or paths to make access easy in all weathers. Crops such as squashes and pumpkins also need a constant supply of water while they are growing, so you should also consider the access to an outdoor tap for your hose or watering can.

Most gardeners prefer to have a rectangular vegetable plot, up to 3.6m/12ft wide and as long as the garden permits. This large plot will usually be divided by a central path, and within the two sub-plots the vegetables will be set out across the beds, in rows or blocks of varying sizes.

In recent years, however, the traditional practice of using deep beds has come back into favour. Each bed is about 1.2m/4ft wide, and any number of individual beds, with a more or less permanent path between, can be used. The significance of the width is that the gardener is able to reach all the crops without having to step on the soil and compact it.

LEFT A large bed of pumpkins and squashes. Bear in mind that such close planting makes harvesting difficult, unless they are all harvested at once.

ABOVE Decorative climbing squashes can be trained over arches and trellises anywhere in the garden.

ABOVE RIGHT These large squashes form a shady walkway in summer. They are ripe and ready for harvesting.

PLANNING THE CROP

Anyone who grows a lot of vegetables will want to dedicate part of the garden to them and to practise a rotational scheme, in which cucurbits (members of the Cucurbitaceae family) can play a useful role. Unlike root vegetables, which should not be planted on recently manured ground, squashes, pumpkins, marrows, courgettes (zucchini) and cucumbers can be planted on ground that was treated with well-rotted manure in spring (indeed, they can even be grown on a manure or compost heap). After harvesting these annual vegetables, the ground can be used for winter root vegetables or onions.

It is also important to remember that plants such as marrows, squashes and pumpkins need a lot of space. Bush marrows need to be 90cm/36in apart, and you should allow up to 1.8m/6ft between trailing forms. Even the smaller outdoor (ridge) cucumbers need to be about 75cm/30in apart, while fairly compact plants, such as gherkins, should be 60cm/24in apart. Trailing forms of marrows and squashes can be grown successfully in more decorative parts of the garden if you train them over pergolas and arches, and this can be the best way to grow these plants if you have only limited room for vegetables.

Growing in the greenhouse

Although it is not essential, a greenhouse will certainly make it easier for you to grow annuals such as pumpkins and squashes, which are raised from seed in spring before being planted outside after the last frost, and if you want to grow indoor cucumbers, you will obviously need a greenhouse. Seeds can, of course, be sown and seedlings brought on in seed trays and pots on indoor windowsills, but this is not always convenient – especially if space in your kitchen is already limited. Moreover, seedlings on windowsills can become drawn and etiolated because the light source is from a single direction, and they can also become scorched before you realize that the sunlight is too bright for the tender first leaves.

PLANNING A GREENHOUSE

Many modern greenhouses have sloping sides, which allow in more light, particularly in winter and early spring when the sun is low,

than the traditional styles, which have vertical sides. You can also get octagonal ones, which are especially suitable for small sites. Whichever style you choose, position the greenhouse where it will receive good light. Lean-to greenhouses, built against a house wall, save space and benefit from the warmth of the wall, but they admit light from a single direction only and can, therefore, result in plants getting drawn.

If your garden is large enough for you to be able to choose its site, position the greenhouse as close to the house as possible so that you can get to it easily in poor weather and in the evening. At the planning stage you should also consider whether you want an electricity cable run to the greenhouse so that you can heat

LEFT Climbing varieties of cucumbers are grown under glass. They have smooth skins and are longer than ridge varieties.

ABOVE This standard straight-sided greenhouse is made of aluminium, but it has been painted green so that it blends in better with the colours of the garden.

it in winter and use a heated propagating tray to get your seeds off to an early start in spring.

HEATING AND VENTILATION

The most versatile means of heating a greenhouse is by electricity. Although the cost of heat may be greater, it is possible to control the output with thermostats, so that little or no heat is wasted because the appliance comes on only when the temperature drops below a certain point. Thermostatically controlled gas heaters are now becoming available. Paraffin heaters are inexpensive, but they need to be filled and maintained regularly. They also produce large amounts of water vapour, which will encourage diseases unless the greenhouse is properly ventilated.

RIGHT It is vital not to let greenhouses overheat. Open the windows during the hottest part of the day, or if you are not at home, automatic window-openers can do the job for you.

Heating bills can be kept down by insulating the greenhouse. Double glazing is excellent but expensive, and it is much more economical to line the greenhouse with sheets of bubble-wrap plastic during winter. If you have only a few plants or seed trays to protect, screen off a section of the greenhouse and heat this small area.

When you buy a greenhouse, make sure that it has as many opening windows as possible to permit the free passage of air right through the structure. Stagnant air encourages insect pests and the development of fungal diseases. If you are at work during the day, it is worth considering having temperature-controlled ventilation fitted, which will make sure that windows and louvres open

BELOW An electric fan heater with a thermostat comes on only when extra heat is required. It can also be used to circulate the air on still, damp days.

automatically on hot days. Good ventilation is important even in winter, so if it is too cold to leave the greenhouse door open, use a fan to keep the air circulating.

SHADING

Although greenhouses need to receive as much light as possible, especially in spring, autumn and winter, in summer the bright sunshine will raise the temperature inside the greenhouse to such an extent that plants cannot survive. The traditional way of providing shade is to apply an opaque wash to the glass. However, it is time-consuming to apply and cannot easily be removed if the weather changes, so is often left in place from late spring to autumn. Some modified washes become transparent when it rains, letting in more light. Shade netting, which can be draped over the outside or clipped to the inside, is easy to remove on dull days.

HAND POLLINATION

Cucumbers, pumpkins and winter squashes bear separate male and female flowers on the same plant. They may be distinguished by the distinct swelling at the base of the female flowers; male flowers are borne on long, straight stems. Bees and other insects generally pollinate the flowers, but in the greenhouse or during cold springs it may be necessary to pollinate by hand.

Remove all the petals from a male flower and simply press it against a female flower.

Alternatively use a clean, soft paintbrush to remove some pollen from the stamens of a male flower and transfer it to the stigma of a female flower.

Sowing in the open

If you have a sheltered garden or live in an area where there are no spring frosts, you might be able to sow the seed of courgettes (zucchini) outdoors in spring. Pumpkins, squashes and marrows need a slightly higher temperature, but in reliably frost-free areas they are worth sowing. Cucumbers, both indoor and outdoor (ridge) varieties, will need to be started off in a greenhouse or on a windowsill.

PREPARING THE SOIL

To give the seeds a good start, prepare the soil carefully. Several weeks before you plan to sow, remove any weeds that have appeared and rake the soil to break it down into a fine tilth. Cloches or movable frames can also be used to warm up the soil and to prevent it from getting too wet in spring downpours. A floating mulch, such as horticultural fleece or even sheets of newspaper, which can be held down with U-shaped lengths of wire or stones, will also help, but may be less effective than sheets of black plastic. The seeds can be sown in X-shaped cuts in the plastic, which can be left in place to act as a weed-suppressing mulch. Remember to water under a permanent mulch before planting. Fleece or woven types of plastic will allow rain through.

SELECTING SEED

Most of the seed that is available these days is of a high quality, especially when it comes from one

of the major suppliers, and the rate of germination is usually good, although, from time to time, a batch may prove to be unsatisfactory. Non-germination is usually due to a factor such as planting into ground that is too wet or too cold.

Many gardeners like to save their own seed, especially if they are growing unusual or heritage varieties. Bought seed, however, is usually of F1 hybrids, which means that the seed is of first-generation plants, obtained by crossing two selected parents. The plants

growing from such seed will be vigorous, uniform and, in the case of vegetables, high yielding. They might also show resistance to particular pests and diseases. The seed collected from such plants, however, will not necessarily come true to type.

SOWING SEED

The conventional way of sowing seeds is in rows, although the average gardener is unlikely to want to have more than two or three courgette plants, each of which can get to 90cm/36in across.

GROWING SQUASHES AND PUMPKINS

It is best to sow the seeds in small seed pots in an electric propagator set at about 23°C/75°F. The seeds should germinate in about six days, and any that have not sprouted within ten days should be thrown away. Once they have germinated, take the pots out of the propagator and keep them in the greenhouse at about 18°C/65°F for about four weeks. Then, from the end of spring, harden them off in a cold frame and gradually open it up to allow more air in each day. When the threat of any late frost is past, you should be able to plant the pumpkins outside.

If you want to train the plants up a pergola or arbour, or a trellis, start doing so as soon as the plants are large enough to tie into position. Once they are 2.5m/8ft long, pinch out the leading shoot to encourage the plant to thicken out. Pumpkins produce both male and female flowers. The female flowers will produce fruit once they are pollinated. It is best to restrict the larger pumpkins to just two fruits and smaller squashes to about five, so pinch out any subsequent young fruits.

Any pumpkins that are not ripe by the time there is the threat of frost should be covered with a cloche, a large sheet of plastic or some horticultural fleece. When they are ready to be cut, use a sharp knife to avoid wrenching or twisting and thus damaging the fruit.

Use a length of garden twine for guidance and a cane or length of wood so that you space the seeds appropriately. If the ground is dry, water the planting hole before sowing the seed at the depth recommended on the packet.

With plants like courgettes that will grow large, it is wasteful to sow seed in a continuous row, as you would with lettuce or carrot seeds. Instead, station sowing is preferable. Sow groups of three seeds together at distances that will be the eventual gap between plants. When they germinate, remove the two weakest plants.

PROTECTING SEED

Speed of germination can be increased by protecting each group of seeds with a cloche which keeps the soil and seed warm. Remove the cloche, just during the daytime at first, once the seed has germinated, and protect the tender young seedlings from slugs.

Newly sown seed and freshly cultivated ground is always attractive to birds, which will enjoy using the fine soil for dust baths, and many will also eat the seeds or seedlings. Protect the seeds by erecting wire-netting guards, or leave the cloches in place until the seedlings have grown large enough to withstand being pulled out by hungry birds.

LABELLING

Before covering the seed with soil, mark the end of the rows with pegs and a label. Once the drill is filled in, it is difficult to see where it is. It may be some time before the seedlings emerge and the row can be easily disturbed by, for example, accidentally hoeing through it. Similarly, it is important to know exactly what you have sown, so the label should bear the name and variety of the vegetable.

SOWING SEED

1 Draw out a shallow drill with the corner of a draw hoe, using a garden line to ensure that it is straight.

2 If the soil is dry, water along the length of the drill and allow it to drain before sowing seed.

3 Station sow the seed along the drill in groups of three, at the recommended distances for the variety.

4 Put a label at the end of the row clearly showing what is in the row. Put a stick or another label at the far end. Do this before filling in the drill.

5 Rake the soil into the drill over the seed. Gently tamp down the soil along the row with the flat of the rake and then lightly rake over.

6 If the soil is heavy and is difficult to break into a fine tilth, draw out the drill and then line it with potting compost (soil mix) before sowing.

Sowing under glass

Germinating seeds under glass is more tedious and time-consuming than sowing direct into the ground, but raising plants in this way has its advantages. It allows the gardener to grow reasonably sized plants that are ready to set out as soon as the weather allows, stealing a march on those sown in the soil by about two weeks. If there are pest problems, such as slugs or birds, the plants are better able to resist them if they are well grown when they are planted out than if they have to fight for their life as soon as they emerge through the soil.

RIGHT A range of pots and trays is available for sowing seed. Clockwise from top left: individual cells, a half tray, plastic pots, a fibrous pot and fibrous modules.

CONTAINERS

Seeds can be sown in a variety of containers. Traditionally they were sown in wooden trays or flats.

Some gardeners prefer to make their own, claiming that they are warmer and that they can be made deeper than the purchased equivalents. Plastic trays have, however, generally replaced the wooden varieties. They can be made of rigid plastic for repeated use or thin, flimsy plastic, to be used only once before being thrown away. Often, however, only a few plants may be required, and it is rather wasteful to sow a whole or half tray. A 9cm/3½in pot is usually sufficient.

Gardeners are increasingly using modular or cellular trays, in which one or two seeds are sown in a small cell. If both germinate, one is removed and the remaining seedling is allowed to develop without having to be pricked out. This method has the advantage of reducing root disturbance.

Even less root disturbance occurs if the seeds are sown in biodegradable fibrous modules. As soon as the seedling is big enough to be planted out, both pot and plant are inserted into the ground, and the pot allows the roots to grow through its sides into the surrounding earth.

SOWING IN POTS

Fill the pot with a good seed compost (soil mix), tap it on the bench, water, and sow from one to three seeds in each pot, depending on the size.

SOWING IN BLOCKS

Fill the cellular block with compost and tap it on the table to firm it down. Water, then sow one or two seeds in each cell. Cover with a light dusting of compost.

SOWING IN TRAYS

1 Fill the seed tray with seed compost and tamp it down lightly to produce a level surface. Water, allow to drain, then sow the seed thinly and evenly across the compost.

2 Cover with a thin layer of compost, lightly firm down, water carefully and label. Labelling is very important because the seedlings of many vegetables look the same.

WATERING IN

Water the trays or pots by standing them in a shallow tray or bowl of water so that the water comes halfway up the container. Remove the tray or pot as soon as the surface of the compost begins to moisten, and allow to drain.

PROPAGATORS

Propagators are glass or transparent plastic boxes that help to keep the seed tray moist and in a warm atmosphere. Some models have cables in them so that the temperature can be controlled. Cheap alternatives can also be made simply by slipping the tray into a plastic bag and removing it when the seeds have germinated. Plastic jars can be cut down to fit over trays or pots.

USING A COLD FRAME

1 Once the trays or pots of pricked-out seedlings are ready to plant out, harden them off by placing in a cold frame which is opened a little wider each day but closed at night, to begin with.

USING A PROPAGATOR

1 Place the containers in a propagator. You can adjust the temperature of heated propagators like this. Seed packets should indicate the best temperature, but you may need to compromise if different seeds need different temperatures.

HEAT

A source of heat is useful for the rapid germination of seeds. It can be provided in the form of a heated propagator, but most seeds will germinate in a warm greenhouse or even within the house.

SOWING SEED

Fill the seed tray with a good quality seed or potting compost (soil mix). Gently firm down and sow the seeds thinly on the surface.

2 Finally leave the lights of the cold frame off altogether so that the plants become accustomed to outside temperatures. Keep an eye on the weather and cover if frost is forecast.

2 This propagator is unheated and should be kept in a warm position in a greenhouse or within the house. Start opening the vents once the seeds have germinated so that they begin the hardening-off process.

Cover the seeds with a thin layer of potting compost and firm down lightly. Water by placing the seed tray in a shallow bowl of water. Once the surface of the compost shows signs of dampness, remove the tray, let it drain, and place it in a propagator or plastic bag. A traditional alternative is to place a sheet of glass over the tray.

SUBSEQUENT TREATMENT

As soon as the seeds begin to germinate, let in air, and after a couple of days remove the cover altogether. If you are using a propagator, turn off the heat, open the vents over a few days and then remove the tray. Once the seedlings are large enough to handle, prick them out into trays, pots or modules. Make sure they are well spaced and keep them watered.

Before planting them out, harden them off in a cold frame, or by bringing them outside for gradually increasing periods of time each day.

Growing organically

As increasing numbers of people become concerned about the levels of artificial insecticides, fungicides and weedkillers used in the commercial production of all vegetables and fruit, organically grown produce is rapidly gaining in popularity. Fruiting vegetables, such as squashes and pumpkins, are ideal crops to grow organically.

ORGANIC GARDENS

Organic gardeners aim to avoid using any artificial chemicals. This can mean tolerating a certain amount of pest damage – though there are a number of non-chemical control methods – but it allows predator populations to build up, so that in time a natural balance is established. Attracting the widest possible range of wildlife is the best way to achieve this – by growing a wide range of plants, putting out food and nest boxes for birds, and if possible by having a pond, which will greatly increase diversity. Companion planting can also reduce some pest attacks – for example, French marigolds (*Tagetes patula*) have been found to deter whitefly in the greenhouse.

Rather than single or double digging the vegetable plot on a regular basis, organic gardeners often prefer the no-dig system. After an initial thorough digging to remove all perennial weed roots and other debris, the soil is gradually built up by the annual addition of mulches of well-rotted compost and manure. Worms and soil-borne organisms take the nutrients down into the soil; the gardener does not dig in the material. Because the ground is not disturbed by digging, the soil is not unnecessarily aerated (which increases the rate at which nutrients can leach out) and the natural layers of soil that develop over time

BELOW Mixing pumpkins with flowers is an increasingly popular idea, especially when limited space makes it difficult to have a dedicated kitchen garden. As well as looking good, flowers will attract many beneficial insects.

are not destroyed. No-dig beds should not be walked on, as this will damage the soil structure, so they need to be accessible from permanent paths, and perhaps made as raised beds.

FERTILIZING THE SOIL

In addition to regular applications of well-rotted compost or manure, organic gardeners often sow green manures in ground that has become vacant. These plants are dug into the ground before they have set seed, to add organic matter. Many types, including alfalfa, beans and red clover, also "fix" nitrogen from the air into the soil, by means of bacteria in their root nodules.

One of the most useful and decorative green manures is the pretty hardy annual, the poached-egg plant (*Limnanthes douglasii*), which can be sown in autumn (when the annual cucurbits have been cleared away) and will produce a good weed-suppressing ground cover of leaves, which can be dug in the following spring, before the flowers appear. This plant will set seed readily, and if it is allowed to grow on the flowers are useful for attracting beneficial hoverflies and bees to the garden.

Cucurbits of all kinds are greedy feeders, and when they are growing in containers or growing bags it is essential to provide additional food. The perennial Russian comfrey (*Symphytum × uplandicum*) is a vigorous plant that can be grown to produce a liquid feed. Once established, plants can be cut back several times a year. The nitrogen- and potassium-rich leaves can be added to the compost heap as an activator or allowed to rot in water to form a smelly but potash-rich feed. Although not as attractive as comfrey, the leaves of nettles (*Urtica dioica*) can also be used to make a good liquid feed, which contains magnesium, sulphur and iron. Young nettle leaves are also useful compost activators. But beware: both comfrey and nettles can be invasive.

BIOLOGICAL CONTROLS

There are a number of useful biological controls now available. In the open garden, a nematode can be watered into the ground to control slugs, and there is also a bacterium, *Bacillus thuringiensis*, which can be sprayed on crops to kill certain caterpillars. Some

ABOVE A "lacewing hotel" provides an area where lacewings – whose larvae eat large quantities of aphids – can live.

controls can only be used in the greenhouse, notably the parasitic wasp *Encarsia formosa*, which is very effective against whitefly, and a predatory mite, *Phytoseiulus persimilis*, which attacks red spider mite.

Biological controls usually work best when the weather is warm, and some are not suitable for indoor use. Introduce them as soon as the first signs of attack are noticed. Be patient and accept that there will be some damage before the biological agent takes effect. When you use biological controls there will always be some pests – they are essential for the predator to continue to breed – but the population will be reduced and any damage should be negligible.

Growing marrows and courgettes

Marrows and courgettes (zucchini) like an open, sunny situation and a rich, moisture-retentive soil with a pH of 5.5–6.8. They can be grown on the compost heap or in a bed that has been heavily manured during the previous autumn. They are frost tender, so plants should not be put outside before the last frosts have passed, unless they are very well protected with cloches or a warm floating mulch.

Plants can be raised under glass by sowing the flat seed edgeways in individual pots or in modules in late spring, or sown directly in the soil in early summer. Germination is speeded up by soaking the seed in water overnight. Seed that has been planted in the open should be covered with a cloche until it has germinated. Sow two seeds at each position and remove the weaker if both germinate. If sowing in the open, it is a good idea to

ABOVE This marrow is being planted in its fibre pot. It has been grown like this to prevent disturbing the roots.

sow some seed in pots as well, in case seedlings are lost to slugs or sudden cold weather.

Bush types can be left to develop, but trailing varieties may need to be trimmed if they get too vigorous. They can be left to trail outwards or trained round in a circle. If they are grown up a trellis

CULTIVATION

Bush
Sowing time: late spring (under glass) to early summer
Sowing or planting distance: 90cm/3ft
Sowing depth: 4cm/1½in
Distance between sown rows: 90cm/3ft
Thinning distance: no need to thin
Harvesting: midsummer onwards

Trailing
Sowing time: late spring (under glass) to early summer
Sowing or planting distance: 1.2–1.8m/4–6ft
Sowing depth: 4cm/1½in
Distance between sown rows: 1.8m/6ft
Thinning distance: no need to thin
Harvesting: midsummer onwards

or other support, the shoots must be tied in. Towards the end of summer remove the tips of each shoot. Keep well watered.

BELOW Marrows and courgettes (zucchini) can be started off in pots. The seeds should be soaked overnight and then planted about 4cm/1½in deep.

BELOW Do not plant courgettes too close together, which will not only make harvesting difficult but will encourage powdery mildew.

ABOVE A female flower on a developing courgette. The fruits are best harvested with the flowers still attached.

HARVESTING

Courgettes are at their most tender when they are about 10cm/4in long, but are still delicious if harvested at any stage up to a small marrow. Both courgettes and marrows can be harvested until the

BELOW To harvest a marrow, cut the stem with a sharp knife, at least 2cm/¾in away from the base of the fruit.

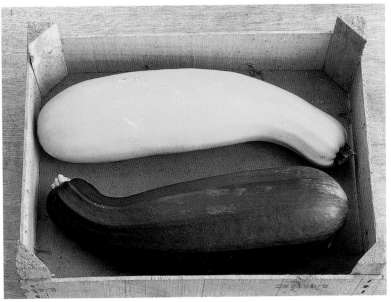

ABOVE If harvested when well ripened, it is possible to store marrows in trays for several weeks.

first frosts. Whatever the size of the crop, cut through the stem 2cm/¾in or more away from the fruit; if closer it will rot. If you want to eat the flowers, which are good raw or cooked, pick the male ones after the females have set.

STORAGE

Courgettes are difficult to store for more than a few days and are best eaten fresh from the plant. They can be frozen, although they become less firm. Marrows, in contrast, will last for several weeks after picking, especially if they have been left to mature and ripen. Pick marrows at the end of the season, before the first frosts, and then store them, so they do not touch, in a frost-free place for several weeks, on trays or hanging in net bags.

PESTS AND DISEASES

Slugs are usually the most severe problem, especially for young plants, eating right through the stem if not checked. Cucumber mosaic virus is the most common disease, causing mottled leaves and distorted fruit. The plant should be burned or destroyed. In some years powdery mildew also occurs, but will not usually cause serious damage.

BELOW Freshly harvested courgettes with their flowers still attached. The flowers can be eaten raw or cooked.

Growing pumpkins

Pumpkins need a sunny site that is open and yet protected from strong winds, which can soon tear the large leaves to shreds. The soil, which should have a pH of 5.5–6.8, should be rich in well-rotted organic material, not only to feed the pumpkins but also to hold plenty of moisture in the soil. At each site, dig a pit 45cm/18in deep and 60cm/24in square and half-fill it with manure before replacing the top soil. Alternatively, they can be grown in a layer of soil on top of a compost heap. In late spring start the pumpkins off in the greenhouse

pumpkin seeds

in modules or fibre pots, at about 15–18°C/59–64°F. You can speed up germination by soaking the seed in water overnight.

When the threat of frost is past, plant in the prepared ground at distances of 1.8m/6ft or further apart for more vigorous varieties. Keep the plant within bounds by

training the stems in a spiral around the plant, pinning them down with wire pegs. If you want to grow giant specimens, reduce the number of young fruits to between one and three. Water regularly and apply a high-potash liquid feed at least once every two weeks – more frequently if you

PLANTING

Pumpkins are greedy feeders and benefit from being planted in a hole line with a thick layer of well-rotted organic material such as manure or compost.

HARVESTING

Pumpkins should be harvested when they have reached their mature colour. Cut them off at the top with a sharp knife, leaving a long stalk if possible.

RIGHT A healthy crop of pumpkins requires an ample supply of water and fertile soil.

want giant fruit for the show bench. Towards the end of summer, pinch out the tips of the shoots. Stop watering and feeding once the fruit is mature.

HARVESTING

Harvest the pumpkins when they have reached their mature colour: deep orange or blue-grey. A good indicator that they are ready is that the stems begin to split. Cut them with a stem about 5cm/2in long. Place them in a sunny position for about a week so that the skins fully harden. Make sure that they are all picked before the first frosts.

BELOW The skins of pumpkins should be hardened in the sunshine.

RIGHT A healthy crop of pumpkins requires an ample supply of water and fertile soil.

STORAGE

After the skins have hardened, orange-skinned pumpkins will store for several weeks in a frost-free position. Blue-grey ones will last much longer, sometimes up to several months. Keep them in a well-ventilated place.

PESTS AND DISEASES

On the whole, pumpkins are trouble-free. Slugs will eat right through the stem if not checked. Cucumber mosaic virus is the most troublesome disease. The leaves become mottled and the fruit distorted. Destroy the entire plant.

Growing squashes

Both summer and winter squashes are cultivated in basically the same way, although winter squashes are often treated like pumpkins, while summer squashes are often regarded as marrows for the purposes of cultivation. Before you decide to grow squashes, remember that the larger varieties are vigorous plants that need a lot of space, although some of those bearing smaller fruits can be trained over an arch or trellis. There are also a lot of named varieties to choose from, so check the details on the packet before you buy.

All squashes need an open, sunny site that is protected from strong winds, which can tear the large leaves. Squashes do best in soil that has a pH of 5.5–6.8 and is rich in organic matter, both to provide them with nutrients and to conserve moisture in the ground.

If you did not dig plenty of well-rotted manure or compost into the ground the previous autumn, prepare a planting hole by removing the soil from an area about 30cm/12in across and 45cm/18in deep. Fill the hole with well-rotted compost or manure and then mound soil over the hole to create a slight dome.

Sow squashes under glass at a temperature of about 18°C/64°F. To avoid root disturbance, which can check their growth, sow the seed into modules or fibre pots. When there is no danger of late frosts, the seedlings can be planted out. Harden the seedlings off carefully before transplanting them. If you have space for more than a single plant, set them 1.8m/6ft apart. Alternatively, in reliably warm, frost-free gardens, they can be sown where they are to grow. Set two or three seeds at each station,

and, when they have germinated, remove the one or two seedlings that are growing less strongly.

CULTIVATION

Summer
Sowing time: late spring (under glass) to early summer
Sowing or planting distance: 1.8m/6ft
Sowing depth: 4cm/1½in
Distance between sown rows: 1.8m/6ft
Thinning distance: no need to thin
Harvesting: late summer and autumn

Winter
Sowing time: late spring (under glass) to early summer
Sowing or planting distance: 1.8m/6ft
Sowing depth: 4cm/1½in
Distance between sown rows: 1.8m/6ft
Thinning distance: no need to thin
Harvesting: autumn

PROVIDING SUPPORT AND PROTECTION

Support growing squashes on straw to prevent them from being attacked by slugs.

Instead of a layer of straw, a terracotta saucer can be used to protect squashes from slugs.

LEFT If necessary, reduce the size of squash plants by cutting off the trailing stems, two leaves above a fruit.

As the stems grow, they can be trained around in a spiral to save space and pinned in place with wire pegs. Varieties that can be grown as climbing plants can be trained up a trellis or netting. Keep the plants well watered and feed with a high-potash liquid fertilizer about once every two weeks, once the plants start to produce flowers and fruit. Squash flowers are usually pollinated by insects, but if your plants are covered in any way or if the fruit does not appear to be setting, you will have to hand pollinate.

HARVESTING

Squashes are ready to harvest when the stems begin to split. Cut the summer squashes when they are large enough to eat and while the skin is still soft (your fingernail should easily sink into the skin). Cut them with a short length of stem attached. Winter squashes can be cut in the same way if they are to be used straight away; for winter storage leave them on the plants for as long as possible, but harvest before the first frosts. If possible, leave in the sun for a few days before storing to harden the skin.

STORAGE

Summer squashes can be stored for a short while – two weeks or so, but generally not much longer. They are best used straight from the plant. If the skins of the winter squashes have been hardened, they will keep for several weeks in a frost-free place. They can be stored in hanging nets or in trays, each squash placed so that it is not touching its neighbour.

PESTS AND DISEASES

On the whole, squashes are usually trouble-free. Slugs are always the most severe problem, and they will quickly eat straight through the stem and make holes in the fruit if they are not checked in time. Cucumber mosaic virus is the most troublesome of the potential diseases. The leaves become mottled and the fruit distorted. The whole plant should be destroyed if it is affected. In some years powdery mildew can also be a problem; it is best to remove affected leaves, but the damage is usually not too serious.

ABOVE Harvest squashes by cutting through the stem with a sharp knife. Winter squashes such as this acorn squash can be left on the plant until needed.

Growing cucumbers

Greenhouse cucumbers need a high temperature, both for germination and throughout the growing season. Using seed of all-female varieties – they are less likely to be bitter – sow two or three seeds, edgeways, in pots or modules and place in a propagator at 24°C/75°F. When they germinate, remove the weaker seedlings and reduce the temperature to 21°C/70°F. Plant the young plants with as little root disturbance as possible into growing bags – an average-sized bag will support two plants. Use square-meshed netting or a system of poles and horizontal wires as supports, and tie in the shoots as they grow. Pinch out the tip of the shoot when it reaches the roof. Tie the laterals to horizontal wires and pinch out the tips two leaves beyond the first fruit to form. Water to keep the soil constantly moist and throw some water on the floor of the greenhouse to keep the atmosphere humid. Keep the greenhouse shaded on very hot days. Once the fruits start to develop, feed them with a high-potash liquid feed every two weeks.

Ridge or outdoor cucumbers need a sunny spot sheltered from the wind. Before sowing, add plenty of well-rotted manure to the soil, which should have a pH of 5.5–7.0. Sow ridge cucumbers either inside in pots or outdoors where they are to grow. If sown directly, cover them with a cloche to raise the temperature. Do not sow until after the threat of frost has passed and the soil has warmed up. Sow, leaving about

CULTIVATION

Greenhouse
Sowing time: late winter onwards
Sowing or planting distance: 60cm/24in
Sowing depth: 2.5cm/1in
Thinning distance: no need to thin
Harvesting: midsummer onwards

Ridge
Sowing time: late spring (under glass) to early summer
Sowing or planting distance: 75cm/30in
Sowing depth: 2.5cm/1in
Distance between sown rows: 75cm/30in
Thinning distance: no need to thin
Harvesting: midsummer onwards

SOWING

Outdoor and greenhouse cucumbers can be sown in mid-spring. Use small pots and fill with a seed-sowing mixture to a little below the rim. Position two or three seeds in each pot, placing them on their narrow edge, cover with compost to a depth of 2.5cm/1in, and water.

THINNING

Keep the pots moist and warm until the seeds germinate. If more than one seed germinates, thin them at an early stage to leave just one seedling in each pot so that it has plenty of space to develop its leaves and a good root system. Remove the weakest seedlings to leave the strongest-growing one.

ABOVE Ridge or outdoor cucumbers growing in the open need a sunny spot that is sheltered from the wind.

75cm/30in in each direction between plants. If the seed is germinated in pots, make sure that the roots are not disturbed when they are transplanted. Fibre pots can help with this, because the cucumbers can be planted without removing them from the pots. Pinch out the tip of the main shoot after six leaves have formed so that the plant bushes out. Water freely. Once the fruits start to develop, feed every two weeks with a high-potash liquid feed.

RIGHT Many modern cucumbers produce only female flowers, but there are some varieties you might grow in a greenhouse that produce both male and female blooms (the female flowers have a small embryo fruit behind the petals). Pinch out male flowers before they have a chance to pollinate the female ones, as this can make the cucumbers less palatable.

RIGHT The most popular type of cucumber is long with a smooth skin, and can only be grown under glass.

HARVESTING
Cut the fruits with a short stalk as soon as they are large enough to eat. Pick frequently and more fruits will develop. Harvest gherkins when they are 5–8cm/ 2–3in long.

STORAGE
Keep for no more more than a few days; they are best eaten fresh.

PESTS AND DISEASES
Slugs and snails can quickly eat through a stem, killing the plant. Cucumber mosaic virus is the most serious disease. In the greenhouse, red spider mite and whitefly may be a problem.

Carving

The sheer variety of their shapes and colours makes squashes and pumpkins a delight to carve. Different types of fruits have varying characteristics which allow for different techniques and styles of carving. Those with very hard flesh are difficult to hollow out and are best simply engraved on the surface; other types, which have scoopable insides but hard skins, can be pierced and drilled; while those with softer skins can be carved in a more intricate manner.

Most of us are familiar with the Hallowe'en tradition of carving ghoulish images in huge orange pumpkins, but the craft need not be limited to these. With a little imagination, you can give many other squash and pumpkin varieties decorative and figurative designs and make glorious seasonal displays for any celebration in the autumn. Indeed, you need not be limited to autumn – you can carve fruits for as long as they are fresh and the flesh is firm enough to cut.

Small night-light candles are often placed inside the hollowed-out shells of carved squashes and pumpkins, providing a warm glow while highlighting the design. The more complicated, delicate patterns are usually cut just into the skin, to become delightful decorations accentuated by the light inside. Simpler shapes can be cut right through the shell so that the brighter beams of light transform the vegetable into an organic lamp. As well as traditional candle night-lights, you can use electric fairy lights or small torches (flashlights), although if a flex is involved you will need to cut a large hole in the underside of the squash or pumpkin and lay the vegetable over the light, rather than leaving the flex to trail untidily out of the top. If using night-lights or candles, make sure that the opening is in the top of the squash or pumpkin and don't cover it with a lid, or else the flesh and skin will burn.

Squashes quickly dry out, and are therefore suitable for making long-lasting decorations or vessels, but pumpkins are fleshy and retain moisture, so once they are cut they will only last for about a week before they begin to moulder. If you are making them for a celebration, do not carve them too soon before the event. The heat of the candles inside them hastens the

LEFT Pumpkin carving is traditionally associated with Hallowe'en, when door steps are aglow with Jack O'Lanterns.

deterioration, so light them at the last moment. The short lifespan of a carved pumpkin makes it all the more special; think of it like a flower arrangement, which you would never expect to last for more than a week. If you want to retain your design for posterity, you can capture it in a photograph.

The fact that squashes and pumpkins soon go off once they are carved does not mean your skills have to be saved up for just a couple of weeks of the year. Kept in a cool place, uncarved, some types of pumpkins will last the year round until the next harvest. Store a good supply when you have harvested them and you will have the raw material for beautiful organic decorations for many months to come.

HOLLOWING OUT

First cut off the lid or bottom of the squash or pumpkin using a large kitchen knife or pumpkin

HOLLOWING OUT A PUMPKIN

1 Cut a circular hole in the top or bottom of the pumpkin with a kitchen knife or pumpkin saw.

2 Hollow out the interior of the pumpkin with a large spoon or ice-cream scoop.

saw. You may also want to level the bottom, if it is to stay intact, so that the vegetable stands firm.

With soft-fleshed pumpkins, hollowing out is easy using kitchen spoons. Firmer flesh can be removed with an ice-cream scoop; hard fruits may have to be hollowed out with the help of a wood-carving tool. Leave the remaining walls 2.5cm/ 1in thick, with a smooth surface to allow the light to shine evenly.

CARVING

Prick out a design on to the surface of the vegetable. Use the correct tool for your pattern: a drill for large holes; a pumpkin saw or small hacksaw for cutting shapes through the surface; and a lino-cutting or woodcarving tool for engraving. When finished, rub the cut areas with vegetable oil to keep them fresh until the squash or pumpkin is ready to be displayed.

CARVING DIFFERENT SHAPES

Drill any holes first. If you are using a large drill bit, first wind it into the pumpkin, then withdraw it by carefully winding back to avoid damaging the edges of the holes.

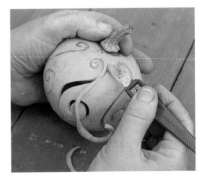

Where you are cutting shapes right through the shell of the pumpkin, use a pumpkin saw or a small hacksaw for hard-skinned pumpkins and a sharp craft knife for those with softer skins.

Designs that are lightly engraved on to the surface of the pumpkin can be cut in much the same way as in lino-cutting, using a selection of lino-cutting or woodcarving tools.

Index

The publisher would like to thank the
following for supplying pictures: *Garden
World Images* 45tl, 46b; *Tim Ellerby* 45tr.